D1309275

CONTENTS

BREAKFAST

QUINOA AND OAT MUESLI
MAKES 6¾ CUPS (ABOUT 12 SERVINGS)

1 cup uncooked quinoa

3 cups old-fashioned oats

¼ cup unsweetened flaked coconut

¾ cup coarsely chopped almonds

½ teaspoon ground cinnamon

½ cup toasted wheat germ

¼ cup ground flaxseeds

1¼ cups chopped dried fruit

1 Preheat oven to 350°F. Spread quinoa in single layer on baking sheet. Bake 8 to 10 minutes until toasted and golden brown, stirring frequently. (Quinoa will make a slight popping sound when almost done.) Remove to large bowl; cool completely.

2 Combine oats, coconut, almonds and cinnamon on same baking sheet; mix well. Spread in even layer. Bake 15 minutes or until mixture is toasted and fragrant but not burnt. Cool completely.

3 Add oat mixture to cooled quinoa in large bowl. Stir in wheat germ, flaxseeds and dried fruit.

GREEK ISLES OMELET

MAKES 2 SERVINGS

1 tablespoon olive oil, divided

¼ cup chopped onion

¼ cup canned artichoke hearts, drained and sliced

¼ cup chopped fresh spinach

¼ cup chopped plum tomato

2 tablespoons sliced pitted black olives, drained

4 eggs

¼ teaspoon salt

⅛ teaspoon black pepper

1 Heat ½ tablespoon oil in small nonstick skillet over medium heat. Add onion; cook and stir 2 minutes or until crisp-tender. Add artichokes; cook and stir until heated through. Gently stir in spinach, tomato and olives; cook 1 minute. Remove to small bowl.

2 Wipe out skillet with paper towels. Add remaining ½ tablespoon oil to skillet; heat over medium heat. Whisk eggs, salt and pepper in medium bowl until well blended.

3 Pour egg mixture into skillet; cook and stir gently, lifting edges to allow uncooked portion to flow underneath. Cook just until set.

4 Spoon vegetable mixture over half of omelet; loosen omelet with spatula and fold in half over filling. Serve immediately.

CARROT CAKE SMOOTHIE
MAKES 1 SERVING

½ cup coconut water

3 medium carrots, peeled and cut into chunks (about 6 ounces)

½ banana

½ cup frozen pineapple chunks

1 teaspoon honey

⅛ teaspoon ground cinnamon

⅛ teaspoon ground ginger

Combine coconut water, carrots, banana, pineapple, honey, cinnamon and ginger in blender; blend until smooth. Serve immediately.

BANANA CHAI SMOOTHIE
MAKES 2 SERVINGS

¾ cup water

¼ cup coconut milk

2 frozen bananas

1 teaspoon honey

¼ teaspoon ground ginger

¼ teaspoon ground cinnamon

¼ teaspoon vanilla

Pinch ground cloves (optional)

Combine water, coconut milk, bananas, honey, ginger, cinnamon, vanilla and cloves, if desired, in blender; blend until smooth. Serve immediately.

CARROT CAKE SMOOTHIE

BLUEBERRY AND BRAN GRANOLA

MAKES 6 TO 8 SERVINGS

½ **cup dried blueberries**

½ **cup finely chopped dried apples**

½ **cup chopped walnuts**

½ **teaspoon ground cinnamon**

½ **teaspoon vanilla**

1 **tablespoon honey**

2½ **cups bran flakes**

1 Preheat oven to 300°F. Spray large rimmed baking sheet or jelly roll pan with nonstick cooking spray.

2 Combine blueberries, apples, walnuts, cinnamon, vanilla and honey in large bowl; mix well. Fold in bran flakes. Spread mixture on prepared baking sheet.

3 Bake about 10 minutes or until mixture is browned and aromatic, stirring halfway through baking time. Cool to room temperature before serving. Store in tightly covered container.

SCRAMBLED TOFU AND POTATOES
MAKES 4 SERVINGS

POTATOES

- ¼ **cup olive oil**
- 4 **red potatoes, cubed**
- ½ **white onion, sliced**
- 1 **tablespoon chopped fresh rosemary**
- 1 **teaspoon coarse salt**

SCRAMBLED TOFU

- ¼ **cup nutritional yeast**
- ½ **teaspoon ground turmeric**
- 2 **tablespoons water**
- 2 **tablespoons soy sauce**
- 1 **package (14 ounces) firm tofu**
- 2 **teaspoons olive oil**
- ½ **cup chopped green bell pepper**
- ½ **cup chopped red onion**

1 For potatoes, preheat oven to 450°F. Pour ¼ cup oil into large cast iron skillet; place skillet in oven 10 minutes to heat.

2 Bring large saucepan of water to a boil. Add potatoes; cook 5 to 7 minutes or until tender. Drain and return to saucepan; stir in white onion, rosemary and salt. Spread mixture in preheated skillet. Bake 25 to 30 minutes or until potatoes are browned, stirring every 10 minutes.

3 For tofu, combine nutritional yeast and turmeric in small bowl. Stir in water and soy sauce until smooth.

4 Cut tofu into large cubes. Gently squeeze out water; loosely crumble tofu into medium bowl. Heat 2 teaspoons oil in large skillet over medium-high heat. Add bell pepper and red onion; cook and stir 2 minutes or until soft but not browned. Add tofu; drizzle with 3 tablespoons nutritional yeast sauce. Cook and stir about 5 minutes or until liquid is evaporated and tofu is heated through. Stir in additional sauce for stronger flavor, if desired.

5 Divide potatoes among four serving plates; top with tofu mixture.

BREAKFAST QUINOA

MAKES 2 SERVINGS

½ **cup uncooked quinoa**

1 **cup water**

1 **tablespoon turbinado sugar**

2 **teaspoons maple syrup**

½ **teaspoon ground cinnamon**

¼ **cup golden raisins (optional)**

Milk (optional)

¼ **cup fresh raspberries**

½ **banana, sliced**

1 Place quinoa in fine-mesh strainer; rinse well under cold water. Transfer to small saucepan.

2 Stir in 1 cup water, sugar, maple syrup and cinnamon; bring to a boil over high heat. Reduce heat to low; cover and simmer 10 to 15 minutes or until quinoa is tender and water is absorbed. Add raisins, if desired, during last 5 minutes of cooking.

3 Serve with milk, if desired; top with raspberries and bananas.

BLACKBERRY LIME SMOOTHIE

MAKES 1 SERVING

½ **cup unsweetened coconut milk**

1 **cup fresh blackberries**

2 **ice cubes**

1 **tablespoon lime juice**

2 **teaspoons honey**

½ **teaspoon grated lime peel**

Combine coconut milk, blackberries, ice, lime juice, honey and lime peel in blender; blend until smooth. Serve immediately.

SPICED PUMPKIN BANANA SMOOTHIE

MAKES 1 SERVING

½ **cup almond milk**

½ **frozen banana**

½ **cup canned pumpkin**

½ **cup ice cubes**

1 **tablespoon honey**

1 **teaspoon ground flaxseeds**

¼ **teaspoon ground cinnamon**

⅛ **teaspoon ground ginger**

Dash ground nutmeg

Combine almond milk, banana, pumpkin, ice, honey, flaxseeds, cinnamon, ginger and nutmeg in blender; blend until smooth. Serve immediately.

BLACKBERRY LIME SMOOTHIE

FARMSTAND FRITTATA

MAKES 4 SERVINGS

1 tablespoon olive oil

1 medium red bell pepper, cut into thin strips, plus additional for garnish

½ cup chopped onion

1 cup cooked broccoli florets

1 cup quartered cooked unpeeled new red potatoes

8 eggs

1 tablespoon chopped fresh parsley

½ teaspoon salt

¼ teaspoon black pepper

½ cup (2 ounces) shredded Cheddar cheese

1 Heat oil in large ovenproof skillet over medium heat. Add 1 bell pepper and onion; cook and stir 3 minutes or until vegetables are crisp-tender. Add broccoli and potatoes; cook and stir 2 minutes or until heated through.

2 Whisk eggs, parsley, salt and black pepper in medium bowl until well blended.

3 Spread vegetables in even layer in skillet. Pour egg mixture over vegetables; cover and cook over medium heat 8 to 10 minutes or until almost set. Meanwhile, preheat broiler.

4 Sprinkle cheese over frittata. Broil 2 to 3 minutes or until set and golden brown. Let stand 5 minutes before cutting into wedges. Garnish with additional bell pepper.

SUPER OATMEAL
MAKES 5 TO 6 SERVINGS

2 cups water

2¾ cups old-fashioned oats

½ cup finely diced dried figs

½ cup sliced almonds, toasted*

⅓ cup turbinado sugar

¼ cup flaxseeds

½ teaspoon salt

½ teaspoon ground cinnamon

2 cups plain unsweetened almond milk or favorite milk, plus additional for serving

*To toast almonds, cook in small skillet over medium heat 2 to 3 minutes or until lightly browned, stirring frequently.

1 Bring water to a boil in large saucepan over high heat. Stir in oats, figs, almonds, sugar, flaxseeds, salt and cinnamon. Add 2 cups almond milk; mix well.

2 Reduce heat to medium; cook 5 to 7 minutes or until oatmeal is thick and creamy, stirring frequently.

3 Spoon into individual bowls. Serve with additional almond milk, if desired.

VEGAN BUTTERMILK PANCAKES

MAKES ABOUT 14 PANCAKES

2 cups plain unsweetened soymilk or other dairy-free milk

2 tablespoons lemon juice

2 tablespoons grapeseed oil

1 tablespoon agave nectar or maple syrup

1 cup all-purpose flour

1 cup spelt flour or whole wheat flour

1 teaspoon baking soda

1 teaspoon baking powder

½ teaspoon salt

1 to 2 tablespoons vegan buttery spread, melted

Fresh fruit and/or maple syrup

1 Combine soymilk and lemon juice in large measuring cup or medium bowl; set aside 5 minutes. Stir in oil and agave.

2 Combine all-purpose flour, spelt flour, baking soda, baking powder and salt in large bowl; mix well. Whisk in soymilk mixture until fairly smooth. (Some lumps will remain.)

3 Heat large nonstick skillet or griddle over medium-high heat. Brush lightly with melted spread.

4 Pour batter into skillet in 4-inch circles. Cook 3 to 5 minutes or until edges of pancakes become dull and bubbles form on tops. Flip pancakes; cook 1 to 2 minutes or until browned. Keep warm. Serve with fruit and/or maple syrup.

GREEN ISLANDER SMOOTHIE

MAKES 2 SERVINGS

2 cups ice cubes

1 banana

1½ cups fresh pineapple chunks

1 cup packed stemmed spinach

1 cup packed stemmed kale

Combine ice, banana, pineapple, spinach and kale in blender; blend until smooth. Serve immediately.

CHERRY ALMOND SMOOTHIE

MAKES 2 SERVINGS

½ cup almond milk

1½ cups frozen dark sweet cherries

½ banana

2 teaspoons almond butter

⅛ teaspoon ground cinnamon

Combine almond milk, cherries, banana, almond butter and cinnamon in blender; blend until smooth. Serve immediately.

GREEN ISLANDER SMOOTHIE

OATMEAL WITH MAPLE-GLAZED APPLES AND CRANBERRIES

MAKES 4 SERVINGS

- 3 **cups water**
- ¼ **teaspoon salt**
- 2 **cups old-fashioned oats**
- 1 **teaspoon butter**
- ¼ **teaspoon ground cinnamon**
- 2 **medium unpeeled red or golden delicious apples, cut into ½-inch pieces**
- 2 **tablespoons maple syrup**
- 4 **tablespoons dried cranberries**

1 Bring water and salt to a boil in large saucepan over high heat. Stir in oats. Reduce heat to medium-low; cook 5 to 6 minutes or until oatmeal is thick and creamy, stirring frequently.

2 Meanwhile, melt butter in large nonstick skillet over medium heat; stir in cinnamon. Add apples; cook 4 to 5 minutes or until tender, stirring occasionally. Stir in maple syrup; cook until heated through.

3 Spoon oatmeal into bowls; top with apple mixture and cranberries.

APPETIZERS AND SNACKS

SWEET POTATO NACHOS

MAKES 4 SERVINGS

2 sweet potatoes
   (1½ pounds total),
   peeled, halved
   lengthwise and
   thinly sliced

1 tablespoon olive oil

   Salt and black pepper

1 can (about 15 ounces)
   black beans, rinsed
   and drained

1 clove garlic, minced

1 teaspoon ancho or
   regular chili powder

¼ teaspoon ground chipotle
   chile (optional)

¼ teaspoon ground cumin

⅛ teaspoon salt

¼ cup water

½ cup (2 ounces) shredded
   Monterey Jack cheese

   Optional toppings: salsa,
   guacamole, sour cream
   and chopped green
   onions

1 Preheat oven to 375°F.

2 Place sweet potatoes in large bowl; drizzle with oil and season with salt and pepper. Toss to coat. Spread on large baking sheet.

3 Bake 30 to 35 minutes or until sweet potatoes are browned and crisp, turning and stirring twice.

4 Meanwhile, combine beans, garlic, chili powder, chipotle chile, if desired, cumin and ⅛ teaspoon salt in medium saucepan; cook over medium heat about 3 minutes or until heated through, mashing some beans with spoon and leaving some whole. Stir in water to make a creamy dip.

5 Spray 8-inch square baking pan with nonstick cooking spray. Spread bean dip in prepared pan. Arrange sweet potatoes around edges of pan; sprinkle with cheese. Bake 5 minutes or until cheese is melted. Serve with desired toppings.

LAVASH CHIPS WITH ARTICHOKE PESTO

MAKES 6 SERVINGS (ABOUT 1½ CUPS PESTO)

3 pieces lavash bread (about 9½ × 7½ inches)

¼ cup plus 2 tablespoons olive oil, divided

¾ teaspoon coarse salt, divided

1 can (14 ounces) artichoke hearts, rinsed and drained

½ cup chopped walnuts, toasted*

¼ cup packed fresh basil leaves

1 clove garlic, minced

2 tablespoons lemon juice

¼ cup grated Parmesan cheese

*To toast walnuts, spread on small baking sheet; bake in preheated 350°F oven 6 to 8 minutes or until golden brown.

1 Preheat oven to 350°F. Line two baking sheets with parchment paper. Position two oven racks in upper third and lower third of oven.

2 Brush both sides of lavash with 2 tablespoons oil; sprinkle with ¼ teaspoon salt. Bake 10 minutes or until lavash is crisp and browned, turning and rotating baking sheets between upper and lower racks after 5 minutes. Cool on wire rack.

3 Combine artichokes, walnuts, basil, garlic, lemon juice and remaining ½ teaspoon salt in food processor; pulse about 12 times or until coarsely chopped. With motor running, slowly add remaining ¼ cup oil and process until smooth. Add cheese; pulse until blended.

4 Break lavash into chips; serve with pesto.

PRESSED PARTY SANDWICH

MAKES 12 SLICES

1 (12-inch) loaf hearty peasant bread or sourdough bread

1½ cups fresh basil leaves

6 ounces thinly sliced smoked provolone or mozzarella cheese (about 9 slices)

3 plum tomatoes, sliced

1 red onion, thinly sliced*

2 roasted red bell peppers

2 to 3 tablespoons extra virgin olive oil

1 tablespoon balsamic vinegar

¼ teaspoon salt

¼ teaspoon black pepper

To reduce the onion's strong flavor, place slices in sieve or colander; rinse with cold water. Shake slices and pat dry.

1 Cut bread in half lengthwise. Place halves cut sides up on work surface. Gently pull out some of interior, leaving at least 1½-inch bread shell.

2 Layer basil, cheese, tomatoes, onion and roasted peppers on bottom half of loaf; drizzle with oil and vinegar. Sprinkle with salt and pepper; cover with top half of loaf.

3 Wrap sandwich tightly in plastic wrap; place on baking sheet. Top with another baking sheet. Place canned goods or heavy pots and pans on top of baking sheet. Refrigerate sandwich several hours or overnight.

4 To serve, remove weights and plastic wrap from sandwich. Cut sandwich into 1-inch slices.

ONION AND WHITE BEAN SPREAD

MAKES ABOUT 1¼ CUPS

- **1 can (about 15 ounces) cannellini or Great Northern beans, rinsed and drained**
- **¼ cup chopped green onions**
- **¼ cup grated Parmesan cheese**
- **¼ cup olive oil, plus additional for serving**
- **1 tablespoon fresh rosemary, chopped**
- **2 cloves garlic, minced**
- **French bread slices**

1 Combine beans, green onions, cheese, ¼ cup oil, rosemary and garlic in food processor; process 30 to 40 seconds or until almost smooth.

2 Spoon bean mixture into serving bowl. Drizzle with additional oil just before serving. Serve with bread.

TIP

For a more rustic-looking spread, place all ingredients in a medium bowl and mash them with a potato masher.

CHICKPEA, ROASTED PEPPER AND OLIVE TOASTS

MAKES 12 SERVINGS

2 cloves garlic, peeled

1 can (about 15 ounces) chickpeas, rinsed and drained

1 cup chopped drained roasted red peppers

¼ cup olive oil

Salt and black pepper

½ cup drained pitted black olives

½ cup drained pimiento-stuffed green olives

24 toasted French bread slices

1 Add garlic to food processor through feed tube with motor running. Add chickpeas and roasted peppers; process until paste forms. Add oil; process until smooth. Transfer to medium bowl; season with salt and black pepper. Cover and let stand 30 minutes.

2 Place black and green olives in clean food processor; pulse until olives are coarsely chopped.

3 Spread 2 tablespoons chickpea mixture on each bread slice; top with 1 tablespoon olive mixture. Serve at room temperature.

NOTE

Leftover chickpea mixture makes a great dip for fresh vegetables.

TIP

Chickpea and olive mixtures can both be prepared up to 2 days in advance. Store separately in airtight containers in the refrigerator.

BEET CHIPS
MAKES 3 SERVINGS

3 medium beets
   (red and/or golden),
   trimmed
1½ tablespoons olive oil
¼ teaspoon salt
¼ teaspoon black pepper

1 Preheat oven to 300°F.

2 Cut beets into very thin slices (about ¹⁄₁₆ inch). Combine beets, oil, salt and pepper in medium bowl; toss gently to coat. Arrange in single layer on baking sheet.

3 Bake 30 to 35 minutes or until darkened and crisp.* Spread on paper towels to cool completely.

*If the beet chips are darkened but not crisp, turn oven off and let chips stand in oven about 10 minutes or until crisp. Do not keep the oven on as the chips will burn easily.

KALE CHIPS
MAKES 6 SERVINGS

1 large bunch kale (about
   1 pound)
1 to 2 tablespoons olive oil
1 teaspoon garlic salt or
   other seasoned salt

1 Preheat oven to 350°F. Line two baking sheets with parchment paper.

2 Wash kale and pat dry with paper towels. Remove and discard center ribs and stems. Cut leaves into 2- to 3-inch-wide pieces.

3 Combine kale, oil and garlic salt in large bowl; toss to coat. Spread on prepared baking sheets.

4 Bake 10 to 15 minutes or until edges are lightly browned and leaves are crisp.* Cool completely on baking sheets. Store in airtight container.

*If the leaves are lightly browned but not crisp, turn oven off and let chips stand in oven about 10 minutes or until crisp. Do not keep the oven on as the chips will burn easily.

BEET CHIPS

BRUSCHETTA
MAKES 8 SERVINGS

4 plum tomatoes, seeded and diced

½ cup packed fresh basil leaves, finely chopped

5 tablespoons olive oil, divided

2 cloves garlic, minced

2 teaspoons finely chopped oil-packed sun-dried tomatoes

¼ teaspoon salt

⅛ teaspoon black pepper

16 slices Italian bread

1 Combine fresh tomatoes, basil, 3 tablespoons oil, garlic, sun-dried tomatoes, salt and pepper in large bowl; mix well. Let stand at room temperature 1 hour to blend flavors.

2 Preheat oven to 375°F. Place bread on baking sheet. Brush remaining 2 tablespoons oil over one side of bread slices.

3 Bake 6 to 8 minutes or until toasted. Top each bread slice with 1 tablespoon tomato mixture.

CAULIFLOWER HUMMUS

MAKES 3 CUPS

2½ teaspoons salt, divided

1 head cauliflower, cut into 1-inch florets

½ clove garlic

¾ cup tahini

2 tablespoons lemon juice

Olive oil and paprika for serving (optional)

Sliced raw fennel and/or bell pepper strips for dipping

1 Fill large saucepan with 1 inch water; bring to a simmer over medium-high heat. Stir in 2 teaspoons salt. Add cauliflower. Reduce heat to medium; cover and cook about 10 minutes or until cauliflower is very tender. Drain and cool slightly.

2 Combine cauliflower, garlic and remaining ½ teaspoon salt in food processor; process 1 minute. Scrape side of bowl. With motor running, add tahini and lemon juice; process 2 minutes or until very smooth and fluffy.

3 Transfer hummus to medium bowl; drizzle with oil and sprinkle with paprika, if desired. Serve with fennel and/or bell pepper strips.

SOCCA (NIÇOISE CHICKPEA PANCAKE)

MAKES 6 SERVINGS

1 cup chickpea flour

¾ teaspoon salt

½ teaspoon black pepper

1 cup water

5 tablespoons olive oil, divided

1½ teaspoons minced fresh basil *or* ½ teaspoon dried basil

1 teaspoon minced fresh rosemary *or* ¼ teaspoon dried rosemary

¼ teaspoon dried thyme

1 Sift chickpea flour into medium bowl; stir in salt and pepper. Gradually whisk in water until smooth. Stir in 2 tablespoons oil. Let stand at least 30 minutes.

2 Preheat oven to 450°F. Place 9- or 10-inch cast iron skillet in oven to heat.

3 Add basil, rosemary and thyme to batter; whisk until smooth. Carefully remove skillet from oven. Add 2 tablespoons oil to skillet, swirling to coat pan evenly. Immediately pour in batter.

4 Bake 12 to 15 minutes or until edge of pancake begins to pull away from side of pan and center is firm. Remove from oven. Preheat broiler.

5 Brush pancake with remaining 1 tablespoon oil. Broil 2 to 4 minutes or until dark brown in spots. Cut into wedges. Serve warm.

NOTE

Socca are pancakes made of chickpea flour that are commonly served in paper cones as a savory street food in the south of France, especially around Nice.

TIP

To make a thinner, softer crêpe, just increase the amount of water in the recipe by about ¼ cup and cook in batches in a skillet.

ROASTED EGGPLANT SPREAD

MAKES 8 TO 10 SERVINGS

1 **eggplant (1 pound)**

1 **medium tomato**

1 **tablespoon lemon juice**

1 **tablespoon chopped fresh basil** *or* **1 teaspoon dried basil**

2 **teaspoons chopped fresh thyme** *or* **¾ teaspoon dried thyme**

1 **clove garlic, minced**

¼ **teaspoon salt**

1 **tablespoon extra virgin olive oil**

Focaccia or pita bread wedges

1 Preheat oven to 400°F. Pierce eggplant with fork in several places.

2 Place eggplant directly on oven rack; roast 10 minutes. Cut off stem of tomato; place in small baking pan. Place tomato in oven with eggplant. Roast eggplant and tomato 40 minutes. Cool vegetables slightly.

3 When cool enough to handle, peel eggplant and tomato. Coarsely chop eggplant.

4 Combine, eggplant, tomato, lemon juice, basil, thyme, garlic and salt in food processor; process until blended. With motor running, slowly add oil and process until well blended. Refrigerate 3 hours or overnight. Serve spread with focaccia.

BEANS AND GREENS CROSTINI
MAKES 12 SERVINGS

4 **tablespoons olive oil, divided**

1 **small onion, thinly sliced**

4 **cups thinly sliced Italian black kale or other dinosaur kale variety**

2 **tablespoons minced garlic, divided**

1 **tablespoon balsamic vinegar**

2 **teaspoons salt, divided**

¼ **teaspoon red pepper flakes**

1 **can (about 15 ounces) cannellini beans, rinsed and drained**

1 **tablespoon chopped fresh rosemary**

24 **toasted baguette slices**

1 Heat 1 tablespoon oil in large skillet over medium heat. Add onion; cook and stir 5 minutes or until softened.

2 Add kale and 1 tablespoon garlic; cook 15 minutes or until kale is softened and most liquid has evaporated, stirring occasionally. Stir in vinegar, 1 teaspoon salt and red pepper flakes.

3 Meanwhile, combine beans, remaining 3 tablespoons oil, 1 tablespoon garlic, 1 teaspoon salt and rosemary in food processor or blender; process until smooth.

4 Spread baguette slices with bean mixture; top with kale.

BLACK BEAN SALSA
MAKES 6 SERVINGS

1 can (about 15 ounces) black beans, rinsed and drained

1 cup frozen corn, thawed

1 tomato, chopped

¼ cup chopped green onions

2 tablespoons chopped fresh cilantro

2 tablespoons lemon juice

1 tablespoon avocado or grapeseed oil

1 teaspoon chili powder

¼ teaspoon salt

6 corn tortillas

Lime wedges and fresh cilantro sprigs (optional)

1 Combine beans, corn, tomato, green onions, chopped cilantro, lemon juice, oil, chili powder and salt in medium bowl; mix well.

2 Preheat oven to 400°F. Cut each tortilla into 8 wedges; place on ungreased baking sheet.

3 Bake 6 to 8 minutes or until edges begin to brown. Cool slightly. Serve tortilla wedges with salsa; garnish with lime wedges and cilantro sprigs.

NOTE
Leftover salsa can be used as a filling for tacos or burritos.

CREAMY CASHEW SPREAD

MAKES ABOUT ½ CUP (6 SERVINGS)

1 **cup raw cashew nuts**

2 **tablespoons lemon juice**

1 **tablespoon tahini**

½ **teaspoon salt**

½ **teaspoon black pepper**

2 **teaspoons minced fresh herbs, such as basil, parsley or oregano**

Assorted bread toasts and/or crackers

1 Rinse cashews and place in medium bowl. Cover with water by at least 2 inches; soak 4 hours or overnight. Drain cashews, reserving soaking water.

2 Combine cashews, 2 tablespoons reserved soaking water, lemon juice, tahini, salt and pepper in food processor or blender; process several minutes or until smooth. Add additional water, 1 tablespoon at a time, until desired consistency is reached.

3 Cover and refrigerate until ready to serve. Stir in herbs just before serving. Serve spread with assorted bread toasts and/or crackers.

TIP

Use this dip as a spread for sandwiches or as a pasta topping. Thin it with additional liquid as needed. You can also use it in place of sour cream as a topping for tacos and chili.

SALADS

BEET AND ARUGULA SALAD
MAKES 6 TO 8 SERVINGS

8 **medium beets (5 to 6 ounces each)**

⅓ **cup red wine vinegar**

¾ **teaspoon salt**

½ **teaspoon black pepper**

3 **tablespoons extra virgin olive oil**

1 **package (5 ounces) baby arugula**

1 **package (4 ounces) goat cheese with garlic and herbs, crumbled**

1 Place beets in large saucepan; add water to cover by 2 inches. Bring to a boil over medium-high heat. Reduce heat to medium-low; cover and simmer 30 minutes or until beets can be easily pierced with tip of knife. Drain well; set aside until cool enough to handle.

2 Meanwhile, whisk vinegar, salt and pepper in large bowl. Slowly add oil in thin steady stream, whisking until well blended. Remove 3 tablespoons dressing to medium bowl.

3 Peel beets and cut into wedges. Add warm beets to large bowl; toss to coat with dressing. Add arugula to medium bowl; toss gently to coat with dressing.

4 Place arugula on platter or plates, top with beets and cheese.

CAULIFLOWER CAPRESE SALAD

MAKES 8 SERVINGS

- **1 head cauliflower, cut into florets and thinly sliced**
- **¾ cup balsamic vinegar**
- **½ cup olive oil**
- **1 teaspoon salt**
- **1 clove garlic, minced**
- **1 teaspoon Italian seasoning**
- **1 container (8 ounces) pearl-shaped fresh mozzarella cheese *or* 1 (8-ounce) ball fresh mozzarella cheese, sliced or chopped**
- **1 pint grape tomatoes, halved *or* 2 cups chopped fresh tomatoes**
- **¼ cup shredded fresh basil**

1 Place cauliflower in large resealable food storage bag or large bowl. Add vinegar, oil, salt, garlic and Italian seasoning. Seal bag; shake to coat. Marinate in refrigerator 8 hours or overnight.

2 Pour cauliflower and marinade into large bowl. Gently stir in cheese, tomatoes and basil.

TIP

Turn leftovers into a great entrée. Cook pasta (any shape) according to package directions; drain and immediately toss with leftover caprese salad. Serve warm or at room temperature.

FARRO, CHICKPEA AND SPINACH SALAD
MAKES 4 TO 6 MAIN-DISH SALADS (OR 8 TO 12 SIDE SALADS)

1 cup uncooked pearled farro

3 cups baby spinach, stemmed

1 medium cucumber, chopped

1 can (about 15 ounces) chickpeas, rinsed and drained

¾ cup pitted kalamata olives

¼ cup extra virgin olive oil

3 tablespoons white or golden balsamic vinegar

1 teaspoon chopped fresh rosemary

1 clove garlic, minced

1 teaspoon salt

⅛ teaspoon red pepper flakes

½ cup crumbled goat or feta cheese

1 Bring 4 cups water to a boil in medium saucepan over high heat. Stir in farro. Reduce heat to low; cook 20 to 25 minutes or until farro is tender. Drain and rinse under cold water until cool.

2 Meanwhile, combine spinach, cucumber, chickpeas, olives, oil, vinegar, rosemary, garlic, salt and red pepper flakes in large bowl. Stir in farro until well blended. Gently stir in cheese.

COLD PEANUT NOODLE AND EDAMAME SALAD

MAKES 4 SERVINGS

- ½ **(8-ounce) package brown rice pad thai noodles**
- 3 **tablespoons soy sauce**
- 2 **tablespoons dark sesame oil**
- 2 **tablespoons unseasoned rice vinegar**
- 1 **tablespoon finely grated fresh ginger**
- 1 **tablespoon creamy peanut butter**
- 1 **tablespoon sriracha or hot chili sauce**
- 2 **teaspoons minced garlic**
- ½ **cup thawed frozen shelled edamame**
- ¼ **cup shredded carrots**
- ¼ **cup sliced green onions**
  Chopped peanuts (optional)

1 Prepare noodles according to package directions for pasta. Rinse under cold water; drain well. Cut noodles into 3-inch lengths. Place in large bowl.

2 Whisk soy sauce, oil, vinegar, ginger, peanut butter, sriracha and garlic in small bowl until smooth and well blended.

3 Pour dressing over noodles; toss gently to coat. Stir in edamame and carrots. Cover and refrigerate at least 30 minutes before serving. Top with green onions and peanuts, if desired.

NOTE

Brown rice pad thai noodles can be found in the Asian section of the supermarket. Regular thin rice noodles or whole wheat spaghetti may be substituted.

SPINACH SALAD WITH POMEGRANATE VINAIGRETTE

MAKES 4 SERVINGS

1 **package (5 ounces) baby spinach**

½ **cup pomegranate seeds (arils)**

¼ **cup crumbled goat cheese**

2 **tablespoons chopped walnuts, toasted***

¼ **cup pomegranate juice**

2 **tablespoons extra virgin olive oil**

1 **tablespoon red wine vinegar**

1 **tablespoon honey**

½ **teaspoon salt**

¼ **teaspoon black pepper**

*To toast walnuts, cook in small skillet over medium heat 1 to 2 minutes or until lightly browned, stirring frequently.

1 Combine spinach, pomegranate seeds, cheese and walnuts in large bowl.

2 Whisk pomegranate juice, oil, vinegar, honey, salt and pepper in small bowl until well blended.

3 Pour dressing over salad; toss gently to coat. Serve immediately.

TIP

For easier removal of pomegranate seeds, cut a pomegranate into pieces and immerse in a bowl of cold water. The membrane that holds the seeds in place will float to the top; discard it and collect the seeds. For convenience, you can find containers of ready-to-use pomegranate seeds in the refrigerated produce section of some supermarkets.

LENTIL AND ORZO PASTA SALAD

MAKES 4 SERVINGS

8 cups water

½ cup dried lentils, rinsed and sorted

4 ounces uncooked orzo

1½ cups quartered cherry tomatoes

¾ cup finely chopped celery

½ cup chopped red onion

2 ounces pitted olives (about 16 olives), coarsely chopped

3½ tablespoons cider vinegar

2½ tablespoons olive oil

1 tablespoon dried basil

1 clove garlic, minced

¼ teaspoon salt

⅛ teaspoon red pepper flakes

4 ounces feta cheese with sun-dried tomatoes and basil

1 Bring water to a boil in large saucepan over high heat. Add lentils; cook 12 minutes.

2 Add orzo to saucepan; cook 10 minutes or just until tender. Drain and rinse lentils and orzo under cold water to cool completely. Drain well.

3 Meanwhile, combine tomatoes, celery, onion, olives, vinegar, oil, basil, garlic, salt and red pepper flakes in large bowl; mix well.

4 Stir lentil mixture into tomato mixture. Gently stir in cheese. Let stand 15 minutes before serving.

CRUNCHY JICAMA, RADISH AND MELON SALAD

MAKES 8 SERVINGS

- 3 **cups thinly cut jicama**
- 3 **cups watermelon cubes**
- 2 **cups cantaloupe cubes**
- 1 **cup sliced radishes**
- 3 **tablespoons chopped fresh cilantro**
- 2 **tablespoons olive oil**
- 2 **tablespoons lime juice**
- 1 **tablespoon orange juice**
- 1 **tablespoon cider vinegar**
- 1 **tablespoon honey**
- ½ **teaspoon salt**

1 Combine jicama, watermelon, cantaloupe and radishes in large bowl.

2 Whisk cilantro, oil, lime juice, orange juice, vinegar, honey and salt in small bowl until well blended.

3 Pour dressing over salad; toss gently to coat. Serve immediately.

WHEAT BERRY APPLE SALAD

MAKES 4 TO 6 SERVINGS

1 cup uncooked wheat berries (whole wheat kernels)

1 teaspoon salt, divided

2 apples (1 red and 1 green)

½ cup dried cranberries

⅓ cup chopped walnuts

1 stalk celery, chopped

Grated peel and juice of 1 medium orange

2 tablespoons rice wine vinegar

1½ tablespoons chopped fresh mint

1 tablespoon extra virgin olive oil

Lettuce leaves (optional)

1 Combine wheat berries and ½ teaspoon salt in large saucepan; cover with 1 inch water.* Bring to a boil over high heat. Stir wheat berries. Reduce heat to low; cover and cook 45 minutes to 1 hour or until wheat berries are tender but chewy, stirring occasionally. (Add additional water if wheat berries become dry during cooking.) Drain and let cool. (Refrigerate up to 4 days if not using immediately.)

2 Cut apples into bite-size pieces. Combine wheat berries, apples, cranberries, walnuts, celery, orange peel, orange juice, vinegar, mint, oil and remaining ½ teaspoon salt in large bowl; mix well. Cover and refrigerate at least 1 hour to allow flavors to blend. Serve on lettuce leaves, if desired.

*To cut cooking time by 20 to 30 minutes, wheat berries may be soaked in water overnight. Drain and cover with 1 inch fresh water before cooking.

SPICY SWEET POTATO SALAD

MAKES 4 TO 6 SERVINGS

2 sweet potatoes
(about 8 ounces)

½ **cup chopped green
onions**

½ **cup chopped red
bell pepper**

½ **cup canned or thawed
frozen corn, drained**

¼ **cup salted peanuts**

2 tablespoons olive oil

1 tablespoon lime juice

⅛ **teaspoon ground red
pepper**

Salt and black pepper

1 Pierce sweet potatoes in several places with fork and place in microwavable dish. Cover loosely with plastic wrap; microwave on HIGH 6 to 7 minutes, turning halfway through cooking. Let stand 10 minutes.

2 Peel sweet potatoes; cut into 1-inch pieces. Transfer to large bowl. Add green onions, bell pepper, corn and peanuts; mix well.

3 Whisk oil, lime juice and ground red pepper in small bowl until well blended. Season with salt and black pepper.

4 Pour dressing over sweet potato mixture; toss to coat. Serve immediately or refrigerate until ready to serve.

ORZO, BLACK BEAN AND EDAMAME SALAD

MAKES 4 SERVINGS

⅔ **cup uncooked orzo**

¾ **cup frozen shelled edamame**

¾ **cup diced carrots**

¾ **cup canned black beans, rinsed and drained**

½ **cup diced green bell pepper**

2 **tablespoons grated Parmesan cheese**

2 **tablespoons finely chopped fresh cilantro**

2 **tablespoons lime juice**

2 **tablespoons extra virgin olive oil**

¼ **teaspoon salt**

⅛ **teaspoon black pepper**

1 Cook orzo according to package directions. About 5 minutes before end of cooking, add edamame and carrots to saucepan; continue cooking until orzo is tender.

2 Drain and transfer to large bowl; stir in beans, bell pepper, cheese and cilantro.

3 Whisk lime juice, oil, salt and black pepper in small bowl until well blended.

4 Pour dressing over salad, toss gently to coat. Serve salad warm or at room temperature.

GREEK LENTIL SALAD WITH FETA VINAIGRETTE

MAKES 3 SERVINGS

- **4 cups water**
- **¾ cup dried lentils, rinsed and sorted**
- **1 bay leaf**
- **¼ cup chopped green onions**
- **1 large stalk celery, chopped**
- **1 cup grape tomatoes, halved**
- **¼ cup crumbled feta cheese**
- **2 tablespoons olive oil**
- **1 tablespoon white wine vinegar**
- **½ teaspoon dried thyme**
- **½ teaspoon dried oregano**
- **½ teaspoon salt**
- **¼ teaspoon black pepper**

1 Combine water, lentils and bay leaf in small saucepan; bring to a boil over high heat. Reduce heat to medium-low; partially cover and cook 40 minutes or until lentils are tender but not mushy.

2 Drain lentils; remove and discard bay leaf. Transfer to medium bowl; stir in green onions, celery and tomatoes.

3 Whisk cheese, oil, vinegar, thyme, oregano, salt and pepper in small bowl until blended.

4 Pour dressing over lentil mixture; stir gently to coat. Let stand at least 10 minutes before serving.

CORN AND ROASTED RED PEPPER RICE SALAD

MAKES 4 SERVINGS

- 3 **tablespoons olive oil, divided**
- 3 **cloves garlic, minced**
- 1 **package (10 ounces) frozen corn, thawed**
- ½ **cup roasted red peppers, drained and chopped**
- 2 **cups cooked brown rice**
- ¼ **cup chopped fresh cilantro**
- ¼ **cup lime juice**
- 1 **teaspoon ground cumin**
- ¼ **teaspoon salt**

1 Heat 1 tablespoon oil in large skillet over medium heat. Add garlic; cook and stir 1 minute.

2 Add corn and roasted peppers; cook and stir 1 minute or until heated through. Transfer to large bowl; add rice and cilantro.

3 Whisk remaining 2 tablespoons oil, lime juice, cumin and salt in small bowl until well blended.

4 Pour dressing over rice mixture; toss gently to coat. Refrigerate 1 hour before serving.

COUSCOUS AND BLACK BEAN SALAD

MAKES 4 SERVINGS

1⅓ cups cooked whole wheat couscous

1 can (about 15 ounces) black beans, rinsed and drained

1 cup cherry tomatoes

2 tablespoons minced fresh chives or green onion (green parts only)

1 tablespoon minced fresh cilantro

1 small jalapeño pepper,* seeded and minced (optional)

2 tablespoons white wine vinegar

1 tablespoon olive oil

¼ teaspoon salt

⅛ teaspoon black pepper

*Jalapeño peppers can sting and irritate the skin, so wear rubber gloves when handling peppers and do not touch your eyes.

1 Combine couscous and beans in large bowl; mix well.

2 Cut tomatoes in half, reserving 1 tablespoon tomato juice. Add tomatoes to couscous. Gently stir in chives, cilantro and jalapeño, if desired.

3 Whisk vinegar, reserved tomato juice, oil, salt and black pepper in small bowl until well blended.

4 Pour dressing over couscous mixture; toss gently to coat.

SOUPS
AND STEWS

CURRIED GINGER PUMPKIN SOUP

MAKES 8 SERVINGS

1 tablespoon olive oil

1 large sweet onion (such as Walla Walla), coarsely chopped

1 large Golden Delicious apple, peeled and coarsely chopped

3 slices (¼-inch) peeled fresh ginger

1½ teaspoons curry powder

2½ to 3 cups vegetable broth, divided

2 cans (15 ounces each) pure pumpkin

1 cup coconut milk

1 teaspoon salt

⅛ teaspoon black pepper

Roasted salted pumpkin seeds (optional)

1 Heat oil in large saucepan over medium heat. Add onion, apple, ginger and curry powder; cook and stir 10 minutes. Add ½ cup broth; cover and cook 10 minutes or until apple is tender.

2 Use hand-held immersion blender to purée mixture until smooth. (Or purée in food processor or blender and return to saucepan.)

3 Stir in pumpkin, 2 cups broth, coconut milk, salt and pepper; cook until heated through, stirring occasionally. If soup is too thick, add additional broth, a few tablespoons at a time, until soup reaches desired consistency. Sprinkle with pumpkin seeds, if desired.

TEX-MEX BLACK BEAN AND CORN STEW

MAKES 4 SERVINGS

1 tablespoon olive oil

1 small onion, chopped

4 cloves garlic, minced

1 teaspoon chili powder

1 teaspoon ground cumin

2 medium zucchini or yellow squash (or 1 of each), cut into ½-inch chunks

1 can (about 15 ounces) black beans, rinsed and drained

1 can (about 14 ounces) fire-roasted diced tomatoes

1 cup frozen corn

¾ cup salsa

½ cup (2 ounces) shredded Cheddar or pepper jack cheese

¼ cup chopped fresh cilantro or green onion

1 Heat oil in large saucepan over medium heat. Add onion; cook and stir 5 minutes. Add garlic, chili powder and cumin; cook and stir 1 minute.

2 Stir in zucchini, beans, tomatoes, corn and salsa; bring to a boil over high heat. Reduce heat to low; cover and cook 20 minutes or until vegetables are tender.

3 Top with cheese and cilantro just before serving.

MINESTRONE SOUP

MAKES 4 TO 6 SERVINGS

1 tablespoon olive oil

½ cup chopped onion

1 stalk celery, diced

1 carrot, diced

2 cloves garlic, minced

4 cups vegetable broth

1 bay leaf

¾ teaspoon salt

½ teaspoon dried basil

½ teaspoon dried oregano

¼ teaspoon dried thyme

   Ground black pepper

1 can (about 15 ounces) dark red kidney beans, rinsed and drained

1 can (about 15 ounces) navy beans, rinsed and drained

1 can (about 14 ounces) diced tomatoes

1 cup diced zucchini

½ cup uncooked small shell pasta

½ cup frozen cut green beans

¼ cup dry red wine

1 cup packed chopped fresh spinach

   Grated Parmesan cheese (optional)

1 Heat oil in large saucepan or Dutch oven over medium-high heat. Add onion, celery, carrot and garlic; cook and stir 5 to 7 minutes or until vegetables are tender. Add broth, bay leaf, salt, basil, oregano, thyme and pepper; bring to a boil.

2 Stir in kidney beans, navy beans, tomatoes, zucchini, pasta, green beans and wine; cook 10 minutes, stirring occasionally.

3 Add spinach; cook 2 minutes or until pasta and zucchini are tender. Remove and discard bay leaf. Garnish with cheese.

GREEN CURRY WITH TOFU

MAKES 2 TO 4 SERVINGS

1 tablespoon grapeseed oil

1 onion, chopped

1 package (14 ounces) firm tofu, drained and cut into 1-inch cubes

⅓ cup Thai green curry paste

1 can (about 13 ounces) coconut milk

1 broccoli crown (about 8 ounces), cut into florets

1 cup cut green beans (1-inch pieces)

½ teaspoon salt

Hot cooked rice or noodles

1 Heat oil in large skillet over high heat. Add onion; cook and stir 5 minutes or until onion is soft and lightly browned.

2 Add tofu and curry paste; cook and stir 2 minutes or until curry is fragrant and tofu is coated. Stir in coconut milk; bring to a boil. Reduce heat to low; stir in broccoli, green beans and salt.

3 Cook 20 minutes or until vegetables are tender and sauce is thickened, stirring frequently. Serve with rice.

PESTO TORTELLINI SOUP
MAKES 6 SERVINGS

1 package (9 ounces) refrigerated cheese tortellini

3 cans (about 14 ounces each) vegetable broth

1 jar (7 ounces) roasted red peppers, drained and thinly sliced

¾ cup frozen green peas

3 to 4 cups packed stemmed fresh spinach

2 tablespoons prepared pesto

Grated Parmesan cheese (optional)

1 Cook tortellini according to package directions; drain.

2 Meanwhile, bring broth to a boil in large saucepan over high heat. Add cooked tortellini, roasted peppers and peas; return to a boil. Reduce heat to medium; cook 1 minute.

3 Remove from heat; stir in spinach and pesto. Serve with cheese, if desired.

MIDDLE EASTERN VEGETABLE STEW

MAKES 6 SERVINGS

¼ cup olive oil

3 cups (12 ounces) sliced zucchini

2 cups (6 ounces) cubed peeled eggplant

2 cups sliced quartered peeled sweet potatoes

1½ cups cubed peeled butternut squash (optional)

1 can (28 ounces) crushed tomatoes

1 cup drained canned chickpeas

½ cup raisins or currants (optional)

1½ teaspoons ground cinnamon

1 teaspoon salt

1 teaspoon grated orange peel

¾ teaspoon ground cumin

½ teaspoon paprika

¼ to ½ teaspoon ground red pepper

⅛ teaspoon ground cardamom

Hot cooked whole wheat couscous or brown rice (optional)

1 Heat oil in large saucepan or Dutch oven over medium heat. Add zucchini, eggplant, sweet potatoes and squash, if desired; cook 8 to 10 minutes until vegetables are slightly softened, stirring frequently.

2 Stir in tomatoes, chickpeas, raisins, if desired, cinnamon, salt, orange peel, cumin, paprika, red pepper and cardamom; bring to a boil over high heat.

3 Reduce heat to low; cover and cook 30 minutes or until vegetables are tender. If sauce becomes too thick, stir in water to thin. Serve stew over couscous, if desired.

BLACK BEAN SOUP

MAKES 4 TO 6 SERVINGS

2 tablespoons olive oil

1 cup diced onion

1 stalk celery, diced

2 carrots, diced

½ small green bell pepper, diced

4 cloves garlic, minced

4 cans (about 15 ounces each) black beans, rinsed and drained, divided

4 cups vegetable broth, divided

2 tablespoons cider vinegar

2 teaspoons chili powder

½ teaspoon salt

½ teaspoon ground red pepper

½ teaspoon ground cumin

¼ teaspoon liquid smoke

Optional toppings: sour cream, chopped green onions and shredded Cheddar cheese

1 Heat oil in large saucepan or Dutch oven over medium-low heat. Add onion, celery, carrots, bell pepper and garlic; cook 10 minutes, stirring occasionally.

2 Combine half of beans and 1 cup broth in food processor or blender; process until smooth. Add to vegetables in saucepan.

3 Stir in remaining beans, 3 cups broth, vinegar, chili powder, salt, red pepper, cumin and liquid smoke; bring to a boil over high heat.

4 Reduce heat to medium-low; cook 1 hour or until vegetables are tender and soup is thickened. Garnish as desired.

LENTIL AND SPINACH STEW

MAKES 4 SERVINGS

- 1 tablespoon olive oil
- 3 medium stalks celery, cut into ½-inch pieces
- 3 medium carrots, cut into ½-inch pieces
- 1 medium onion, chopped
- 3 cloves garlic, minced
- 4 cups vegetable broth
- 1 can (about 14 ounces) diced tomatoes
- 1 cup dried lentils, rinsed and sorted
- 2 teaspoons ground cumin
- ½ teaspoon dried basil
- ½ teaspoon salt
- ¼ teaspoon black pepper
- 5 cups baby spinach
- 3 cups hot cooked ditalini pasta

SLOW COOKER DIRECTIONS

1 Heat oil in large skillet over medium-high heat. Add celery, carrots, onion and garlic; cook and stir 3 to 4 minutes or until vegetables begin to soften.

2 Transfer vegetable mixture to slow cooker. Stir in broth, tomatoes, lentils, cumin, basil, salt and pepper; mix well.

3 Cover; cook on LOW 8 to 9 hours or until lentils are tender but still hold their shape. Stir in spinach just before serving. Serve over pasta.

BUTTERNUT BISQUE

MAKES 4 TO 6 SERVINGS

1 tablespoon butter or olive oil

1 large onion, coarsely chopped

1 medium butternut squash (about 1½ pounds), cut into ½-inch pieces

2 cans (about 14 ounces each) vegetable broth, divided

½ teaspoon salt

¼ teaspoon ground nutmeg

⅛ teaspoon white pepper

Plain yogurt and chopped fresh chives (optional)

1 Melt butter in large saucepan over medium heat. Add onion; cook and stir 3 minutes. Add squash, 1 can broth and salt; bring to a boil over high heat. Reduce heat to low; cover and simmer 20 minutes or until squash is very tender.

2 Use hand-held immersion blender to purée soup until smooth. (Or purée soup in batches in food processor or blender and return to saucepan.)

3 Stir in remaining can of broth, nutmeg and pepper; cook, uncovered, 5 minutes, stirring occasionally. Top with yogurt and chives, if desired.

HEARTY VEGETABLE STEW

MAKES 6 TO 8 SERVINGS

1 tablespoon olive oil

1 cup chopped onion

¾ cup chopped carrots

3 cloves garlic, minced

4 cups coarsely chopped green cabbage

3½ cups coarsely chopped unpeeled new red potatoes

1 teaspoon salt

1 teaspoon dried rosemary

½ teaspoon black pepper

4 cups vegetable broth

1 can (about 15 ounces) Great Northern beans, rinsed and drained

1 can (about 14 ounces) diced tomatoes

Grated Parmesan cheese (optional)

1 Heat oil in large saucepan or Dutch oven over medium-high heat. Add onion and carrots; cook and stir 3 minutes. Add garlic; cook and stir 1 minute.

2 Stir in cabbage, potatoes, salt, rosemary and pepper; cook 1 minute. Stir in broth, beans and tomatoes; bring to a boil.

3 Reduce heat to medium-low; cook 15 minutes or until potatoes are tender. Serve with cheese, if desired.

HOT AND SOUR SOUP WITH BOK CHOY AND TOFU

MAKES 4 SERVINGS

1 tablespoon dark sesame oil

4 ounces fresh shiitake mushrooms, stems finely chopped, caps thinly sliced

2 cloves garlic, minced

2 cups mushroom broth or vegetable broth

1 cup plus 2 tablespoons cold water, divided

2 tablespoons reduced-sodium soy sauce

1½ tablespoons rice vinegar or white wine vinegar

¼ teaspoon red pepper flakes

1½ tablespoons cornstarch

2 cups coarsely chopped bok choy leaves or napa cabbage

10 ounces silken extra firm tofu, well drained, cut into ½-inch cubes

1 green onion, thinly sliced

1 Heat oil in large saucepan over medium heat. Add mushrooms and garlic; cook and stir 3 minutes. Add broth, 1 cup water, soy sauce, vinegar and red pepper flakes; bring to a boil. Reduce heat to medium-low; cook 5 minutes.

2 Stir remaining 2 tablespoons water into cornstarch in small bowl until smooth. Whisk into soup; cook 2 minutes or until thickened.

3 Stir in bok choy; cook 2 to 3 minutes or until wilted. Stir in tofu; cook until heated through. Top with green onion.

MEDITERRANEAN EGGPLANT AND WHITE BEAN STEW
MAKES 6 SERVINGS

1 tablespoon olive oil

1 medium onion, chopped

1 medium eggplant (1 pound), peeled and cut into ¾-inch pieces

4 cloves garlic, minced

1 can (28 ounces) stewed tomatoes, undrained

2 bell peppers (1 red and 1 yellow), cut into ¾-inch pieces

1 teaspoon dried oregano

¼ teaspoon red pepper flakes (optional)

1 can (about 15 ounces) Great Northern or cannellini beans, rinsed and drained

¼ cup grated Parmesan cheese

¼ cup chopped fresh basil

1 Heat oil in large saucepan or Dutch oven over medium heat. Add onion; cook and stir 5 minutes. Add eggplant and garlic; cook and stir 5 minutes.

2 Stir in tomatoes, bell peppers, oregano and red pepper flakes, if desired. Reduce heat to medium-low; cover and cook 20 minutes or until vegetables are tender.

3 Stir in beans; cook, uncovered, 5 minutes. Top with cheese and basil.

SPICY LENTIL AND PASTA SOUP

MAKES 6 SERVINGS

- **1 tablespoon olive oil**
- **2 medium onions, thinly sliced**
- **½ cup chopped carrot**
- **½ cup chopped celery**
- **½ cup peeled and chopped turnip**
- **1 small jalapeño pepper,* finely chopped**
- **2 cans (about 14 ounces each) vegetable broth**
- **2 cups water**
- **1 can (about 14 ounces) stewed tomatoes**
- **8 ounces dried lentils, rinsed and sorted**
- **2 teaspoons chili powder**
- **½ teaspoon dried oregano**
- **3 ounces uncooked whole wheat spaghetti, broken**
- **½ teaspoon salt**
- **¼ cup minced fresh cilantro**

*Jalapeño peppers can sting and irritate the skin, so wear rubber gloves when handling peppers and do not touch your eyes.

1 Heat oil in large saucepan over medium heat. Add onions, carrot, celery, turnip and jalapeño; cook and stir 10 minutes or until vegetables are crisp-tender.

2 Add broth, water, tomatoes, lentils, chili powder and oregano; bring to a boil. Reduce heat to medium-low; cover and cook 20 to 30 minutes or until lentils are tender.

3 Add pasta and salt; cook 10 minutes or until pasta is tender. Sprinkle with cilantro just before serving.

CURRIED VEGETABLE AND CASHEW STEW
MAKES 6 SERVINGS

2 medium potatoes, peeled and cut into ½-inch pieces

1 can (about 15 ounces) chickpeas, rinsed and drained

1 can (about 14 ounces) diced tomatoes

12 ounces eggplant, cut into ½-inch pieces

1 medium onion, chopped

1 cup vegetable broth

2 tablespoons quick cooking tapioca

2 teaspoons grated fresh ginger

2 teaspoons curry powder

½ teaspoon salt

¼ teaspoon black pepper

1 medium zucchini (about 8 ounces), cut into ½-inch pieces

½ cup frozen peas

1 cup golden raisins

½ cup salted cashew nuts

SLOW COOKER DIRECTIONS

1 Combine potatoes, chickpeas, tomatoes, eggplant, onion, broth, tapioca, ginger, curry powder, salt and pepper in slow cooker; mix well.

2 Cover; cook on LOW 8 to 9 hours. Stir in zucchini, peas, raisins and cashews. Turn slow cooker to HIGH. Cover; cook 30 minutes or until zucchini is tender.

PASTA AND GRAINS

HARICOTS VERTS AND GOAT CHEESE QUINOA

MAKES 6 SERVINGS

- **1 cup tri-colored uncooked quinoa**
- **2 cups vegetable broth**
- **½ teaspoon salt, divided**
- **1 tablespoon chopped fresh rosemary**
- **1 package (12 ounces) fresh haricots verts, cut in half**
- **3 tablespoons olive oil**
- **1 tablespoon Dijon mustard**
- **1 teaspoon honey**
- **1 tablespoon lemon juice**
- **⅛ teaspoon black pepper**
- **½ cup toasted pecan pieces**
- **1 container (4 ounces) goat cheese crumbles**

1 Place quinoa in fine-mesh strainer; rinse well under cold water.

2 Combine quinoa, broth and ¼ teaspoon salt in medium saucepan; bring to a boil over high heat. Reduce heat to low; cover and simmer 15 to 20 minutes or until quinoa is tender and broth is absorbed. Add rosemary and haricots verts during last 5 minutes of cooking. Remove from heat; cool to room temperature.

3 Meanwhile, whisk oil, mustard, honey, lemon juice, remaining ¼ teaspoon salt and pepper in small bowl until well blended.

4 Place cooled quinoa mixture in large bowl. Add dressing and pecans; toss to coat. Sprinkle with goat cheese just before serving.

PESTO CAVATAPPI
MAKES 4 TO 6 SERVINGS

PESTO

- **2 cups packed fresh basil leaves***
- **1 cup walnuts, toasted**
- **½ cup shredded Parmesan cheese**
- **4 cloves garlic**
- **1 teaspoon salt**
- **¼ teaspoon black pepper**
- **¾ cup extra virgin olive oil**

PASTA

- **1 package (16 ounces) uncooked cavatappi pasta**
- **1 tablespoon extra virgin olive oil**
- **2 plum tomatoes, diced (1½ cups)**
- **1 package (8 ounces) sliced mushrooms**
- **¼ cup dry white wine**
- **¼ cup vegetable broth**
- **¼ cup whipping cream**

Or substitute 1 cup packed fresh parsley leaves for half of basil.

1 For pesto, combine basil, walnuts, cheese, garlic, salt and pepper in food processor; pulse until coarsely chopped. With motor running, add ¾ cup oil in thin, steady stream; process until well blended. Measure 1 cup pesto for pasta; reserve remaining pesto for another use.

2 Cook pasta in large saucepan of boiling salted water according to package directions until al dente. Drain and return to saucepan; keep warm.

3 Meanwhile, heat 1 tablespoon oil in large skillet over medium-high heat. Add tomatoes and mushrooms; cook about 7 minutes or until most of liquid has evaporated, stirring occasionally. Add wine, broth and cream; bring to a boil. Reduce heat to low; cook about 4 minutes or until sauce has thickened slightly. Stir in 1 cup pesto; cook just until heated through.

4 Pour sauce over pasta; stir gently to coat.

PUMPKIN RISOTTO

MAKES 4 SERVINGS

4 cups vegetable broth

5 whole fresh sage leaves

¼ teaspoon ground nutmeg

2 tablespoons butter

1 tablespoon olive oil

1 onion, finely chopped

2 cloves garlic, minced

1½ cups uncooked arborio rice

½ cup dry white wine

1 teaspoon salt

Black pepper

1 can (15 ounces) pure pumpkin

½ cup shredded Parmesan cheese, plus additional for serving

2 tablespoons chopped fresh sage, divided

¼ cup roasted pumpkin seeds (pepitas) or chopped toasted walnuts or pecans

1 Combine broth, whole sage leaves and nutmeg in small saucepan; bring to a boil over high heat. Reduce heat to low to maintain a simmer.

2 Heat butter and oil in large saucepan over medium-high heat. Add onion; cook and stir 5 minutes or until softened. Add garlic; cook and stir 30 seconds. Add rice; cook 2 to 3 minutes or until rice appears translucent, stirring frequently to coat with butter. Add wine, salt and pepper; cook until most of liquid is absorbed.

3 Add broth mixture, ½ cup at a time, stirring frequently until broth is absorbed before adding next ½ cup (discard whole sage leaves). Stir in pumpkin when about 1 cup broth remains. Add remaining broth; cook until rice is al dente, stirring constantly.

4 Remove from heat; stir in ½ cup cheese and 1 tablespoon chopped sage. Cover and let stand 5 minutes. Top each serving with 1 tablespoon pumpkin seeds and remaining chopped sage. Serve with additional cheese, if desired.

QUINOA PATTIES WITH ROASTED RED PEPPER SAUCE
MAKES 6 SERVINGS

1 cup uncooked quinoa

2 cups water

1 jar (12 ounces) roasted red peppers, drained

1 tablespoon balsamic vinegar

1 teaspoon lemon juice

1 teaspoon honey

1 clove garlic

4 eggs, beaten

1 cup Italian-style dry bread crumbs

⅓ cup grated Parmesan cheese

2 tablespoons chopped fresh parsley

2 cloves garlic, minced

½ teaspoon salt

1 to 2 tablespoons olive oil

1 Place quinoa in fine-mesh strainer; rinse well under cold water.

2 Bring 2 cups water in medium saucepan to a boil over high heat; stir in quinoa. Reduce heat to low; cover and simmer 10 to 15 minutes or until quinoa is tender and water is absorbed. Cool slightly.

3 Meanwhile, combine roasted peppers, vinegar, lemon juice, honey and garlic clove in blender or food processor; blend until smooth. Set aside.

4 Combine quinoa, eggs, bread crumbs, cheese, parsley, minced garlic and salt in large bowl; mix well. Shape into 12 (¼-cup) patties.

5 Heat 1 tablespoon oil in large skillet over medium heat. Add 6 patties; cook 5 to 7 minutes or until bottoms are browned. Turn and cook 5 to 7 minutes or until browned. Repeat with remaining patties, adding additional 1 tablespoon oil, if necessary. Serve patties with red pepper sauce.

VARIATION
Make 24 mini quinoa patties as an appetizer.

SESAME NOODLES

MAKES 6 TO 8 SERVINGS

1 package (16 ounces) uncooked spaghetti

6 tablespoons soy sauce

5 tablespoons dark sesame oil

2 tablespoons coconut sugar

3 tablespoons rice vinegar

3 cloves garlic, minced

1 teaspoon grated fresh ginger

½ teaspoon sriracha sauce

2 green onions, sliced

1 red bell pepper

1 cucumber

1 carrot

Sesame seeds (optional)

1 Cook spaghetti in large saucepan of boiling salted water according to package directions until al dente. Drain, reserving 2 tablespoons pasta cooking water.

2 Whisk soy sauce, sesame oil, sugar, vinegar, garlic, ginger, sriracha and reserved pasta water in large bowl until well blended. Stir in noodles and green onions. Let stand at least 30 minutes until noodles have cooled to room temperature and most of sauce is absorbed, stirring occasionally.

3 Meanwhile, cut bell pepper into thin strips. Peel cucumber and carrot and shred with julienne peeler into long strands or cut into thin strips. Stir into noodles. Serve at room temperature or refrigerate until ready to serve. Top with sesame seeds, if desired.

FARRO VEGGIE BURGERS

MAKES 6 SERVINGS

1½ **cups water**

½ **cup pearled farro**

¾ **teaspoon salt, divided**

2 **medium potatoes, peeled and quartered**

2 **to 4 tablespoons olive oil, divided**

¾ **cup finely chopped green onions**

1 **cup grated carrots**

2 **teaspoons grated fresh ginger**

2 **tablespoons ground almonds**

¼ **teaspoon black pepper**

½ **cup panko bread crumbs**

6 **whole wheat hamburger buns**

Lettuce, ketchup and mustard (optional)

1 Combine 1½ cups water, farro and ¼ teaspoon salt in medium saucepan; bring to a boil over high heat. Reduce heat to low; partially cover and cook 25 to 30 minutes or until farro is tender. Drain and cool. (If using spelt, use 2 cups of water and cook until tender.)

2 Meanwhile, place potatoes in large saucepan; cover with water. Bring to a boil over high heat. Reduce heat to low; cook 20 minutes or until tender. Drain, cool and mash potatoes; set aside.

3 Heat 1 tablespoon oil in medium skillet over medium-high heat. Add green onions; cook and stir 1 minute. Add carrots and ginger; cover and cook 2 to 3 minutes or until carrots are tender. Transfer to large bowl; cool completely.

4 Add mashed potatoes and farro to carrot mixture. Add almonds, remaining ½ teaspoon salt and pepper; mix well. Shape mixture into 6 patties. Spread panko on medium plate; coat patties with panko.

5 Heat 1 tablespoon oil in large nonstick skillet over medium heat. Cook patties about 4 minutes per side or until golden brown, adding additional oil as needed. Serve on buns with desired condiments.

VEGETARIAN QUINOA CHILI

MAKES 4 TO 6 SERVINGS

2 tablespoons olive oil

1 large onion

1 red bell pepper, diced

1 large carrot, peeled
   and diced

1 stalk celery, diced

1 jalapeño pepper,* seeded
   and finely chopped

1 tablespoon minced garlic

3 tablespoons chili powder

2 teaspoons ground cumin

1 teaspoon salt

1 can (about 15 ounces)
   kidney beans, rinsed
   and drained

1 can (28 ounces) crushed
   tomatoes

1 cup water

1 cup fresh or frozen corn

½ cup uncooked quinoa,
   rinsed well

Optional toppings: diced
   avocado, shredded
   Cheddar cheese and
   sliced green onions

*Jalapeño peppers can sting and
irritate the skin, so wear rubber
gloves when handling peppers
and do not touch your eyes.

1 Heat oil in large saucepan over medium-high heat. Add onion, bell pepper, carrot and celery; cook about 10 minutes or until vegetables are softened, stirring occasionally. Add jalapeño, garlic, chili powder, cumin and salt; cook about 1 minute or until fragrant.

2 Stir in beans, tomatoes, water, corn and quinoa; bring to a boil. Reduce heat to low; cover and cook 1 hour, stirring occasionally.

3 Serve chili with desired toppings.

BULGUR PILAF WITH CARAMELIZED ONIONS AND KALE

MAKES 4 SERVINGS

1 tablespoon olive oil

1 onion, cut into thin wedges

1 clove garlic, minced

2 cups chopped kale

2 cups vegetable broth

¾ cup medium grain bulgur

½ teaspoon salt

¼ teaspoon black pepper

1 Heat oil in large nonstick skillet over medium heat. Add onion; cook about 8 minutes or until softened and lightly browned, stirring occasionally. Add garlic; cook and stir 1 minute. Add kale; cook and stir about 1 minute or until kale is wilted.

2 Stir in broth, bulgur, salt and pepper; bring to a boil. Reduce heat to low; cover and cook 12 minutes or until liquid is absorbed and bulgur is tender.

WHOLE WHEAT SPAGHETTI WITH ROASTED PEPPER TOMATO SAUCE

MAKES 4 SERVINGS

3 red bell peppers

1½ tablespoons olive oil

1 medium red onion, finely chopped

1 clove garlic, minced

1 can (about 14 ounces) fire-roasted diced tomatoes

½ teaspoon salt

¼ teaspoon dried oregano

¼ teaspoon red pepper flakes

⅛ teaspoon black pepper

8 ounces whole wheat spaghetti, cooked and drained

½ cup grated Parmesan cheese

1 Place bell peppers on rack in broiler pan 3 to 5 inches from heat source or hold over open gas flame on long-handled metal fork. Turn bell peppers often until blistered and charred on all sides. Transfer to large bowl; cover and let stand 15 to 20 minutes to loosen skins. Remove skins with paring knife. Cut off tops and scrape out seeds. Chop peppers.

2 Heat oil in large skillet over medium-high heat. Add onion and garlic; cook and stir 3 to 5 minutes or until tender. Add roasted peppers; cook 2 minutes.

3 Stir in tomatoes, salt, oregano, red pepper flakes and black pepper. Reduce heat to low; cook 10 minutes, stirring occasionally.

4 Serve sauce over spaghetti; sprinkle with cheese.

VEGGIE SUSHI ROLLS

MAKES 24 PIECES (ABOUT 4 SERVINGS)

2 tablespoons unseasoned rice vinegar

1 teaspoon sugar

½ teaspoon salt

2 cups cooked short grain brown rice

4 sheets sushi nori

1 teaspoon toasted sesame seeds

½ English cucumber, cut into ¼-inch strips

½ red bell pepper, cut into ¼-inch strips

½ ripe avocado, cut into ½-inch pieces

Pickled ginger and wasabi paste (optional)

1 Combine vinegar, sugar and salt in large bowl; mix well. Stir in rice. Cover with damp towel until ready to use.

2 Prepare small bowl with water and splash of vinegar to rinse fingers and prevent rice from sticking while working. Place 1 sheet of nori horizontally on bamboo sushi mat or waxed or parchment paper, rough side up. Using wet fingers, spread about ½ cup rice evenly over nori, leaving 1-inch border along bottom edge. Sprinkle rice with ¼ teaspoon sesame seeds. Place one fourth of cucumber, bell pepper and avocado on top of rice.

3 Pick up edge of mat nearest you. Roll mat forward, wrapping rice around fillings and pressing gently to form log; press gently to seal. Place roll on cutting board, seam side down. Repeat with remaining nori and fillings.

4 Slice each roll into 6 pieces with sharp knife.* Cut off ends. Serve with pickled ginger and wasabi, if desired.

Wipe knife with damp cloth between cuts, if necessary.

QUINOA BURRITO BOWLS

MAKES 4 SERVINGS

1 cup uncooked quinoa

2 cups water

½ teaspoon salt, divided

2 tablespoons fresh lime juice, divided

¼ cup sour cream or plain Greek yogurt

2 teaspoons vegetable oil

1 small onion, diced

1 red bell pepper, diced

1 clove garlic, minced

½ cup canned black beans, rinsed and drained

½ cup thawed frozen corn

Shredded lettuce

1 Place quinoa in fine-mesh strainer; rinse well under cold running water. Bring 2 cups water to a boil in small saucepan; stir in quinoa and ¼ teaspoon salt. Reduce heat to low; cover and simmer 10 to 15 minutes or until quinoa is tender and water is absorbed. Stir in 1 tablespoon lime juice.

2 Combine sour cream and remaining 1 tablespoon lime juice in small bowl; set aside.

3 Meanwhile, heat oil in large skillet over medium heat. Add onion and bell pepper; cook and stir 5 minutes or until softened. Add garlic; cook 1 minute. Add black beans, corn and remaining ¼ teaspoon salt; cook 3 to 5 minutes or until heated through.

4 Divide quinoa among serving bowls; top with black bean mixture, lettuce and sour cream mixture.

PASTA WITH ONIONS AND GOAT CHEESE

MAKES 6 SERVINGS

1 tablespoon olive oil

3 to 4 cups thinly sliced sweet onions

¾ cup (3 ounces) crumbled goat cheese

¼ cup milk

8 ounces uncooked campanelle or farfalle pasta

1 clove garlic, minced

2 tablespoons dry white wine or vegetable broth

1½ teaspoons chopped fresh sage *or* ½ teaspoon dried sage

½ teaspoon salt

¼ teaspoon black pepper

2 tablespoons chopped toasted walnuts*

To toast walnuts, cook in small skillet over medium heat 1 to 2 minutes or until lightly browned, stirring frequently.

1 Heat oil in large nonstick skillet over medium heat. Add onions; cook 20 to 25 minutes or until golden and caramelized, stirring occasionally.

2 Combine goat cheese and milk in small bowl; stir until well blended.

3 Cook pasta according to package directions; drain.

4 Add garlic to onions in skillet; cook about 3 minutes or until softened. Add wine, sage, salt and pepper; cook until liquid has evaporated. Remove from heat. Add pasta and goat cheese mixture; stir gently until cheese is melted. Sprinkle with walnuts.

WINTER SQUASH RISOTTO
MAKES 4 TO 6 SERVINGS

4 to 5 cups vegetable broth

2 tablespoons olive oil

1 small butternut squash or medium delicata squash, peeled and cut into 1-inch pieces (about 2 cups)

1 large shallot or small onion, finely chopped

½ teaspoon paprika

¼ teaspoon dried thyme

¼ teaspoon salt

¼ teaspoon black pepper

1 cup uncooked arborio rice

¼ cup dry white wine (optional)

½ cup grated Parmesan or Romano cheese

1 Bring broth to a simmer in small saucepan over high heat. Reduce heat to low to maintain a simmer.

2 Heat oil in large nonstick skillet over medium heat. Add squash; cook and stir 3 minutes. Add shallot; cook and stir 3 to 4 minutes or until squash is almost tender. Stir in paprika, thyme, salt and pepper. Add rice; stir to coat.

3 Add wine, if desired; cook and stir until wine is absorbed. Add broth, ½ cup at a time, stirring frequently until broth is absorbed before adding next ½ cup. Continue adding broth and stirring until rice is tender and mixture is creamy, 20 to 25 minutes. Stir in cheese.

SOBA STIR-FRY
MAKES 4 SERVINGS

8 ounces uncooked soba (buckwheat) noodles

1 tablespoon grapeseed oil

2 cups sliced shiitake mushrooms

1 medium red bell pepper, cut into thin strips

2 whole dried red chiles *or* ¼ teaspoon red pepper flakes

1 clove garlic, minced

2 cups shredded napa cabbage

½ cup vegetable broth

2 tablespoons tamari or soy sauce

1 tablespoon rice wine or dry sherry

2 teaspoons cornstarch

1 package (14 ounces) firm tofu, drained and cut into 1-inch cubes

Salt and black pepper

2 green onions, thinly sliced

1 Bring large saucepan of salted water to a boil. Add noodles; return to a boil. Reduce heat to low; cook 3 minutes or until tender. Drain and rinse under cold water to cool.

2 Heat oil in large nonstick skillet or wok over medium-high heat. Add mushrooms, bell pepper, dried chiles and garlic; cook and stir 3 minutes or until mushrooms are tender. Add cabbage; cover and cook 2 minutes or until cabbage is wilted.

3 Stir broth, tamari and rice wine into cornstarch in small bowl until smooth. Whisk sauce into vegetable mixture; cook 2 minutes or until sauce is thickened.

4 Stir tofu and noodles into vegetable mixture; toss gently until heated through. Season with salt and black pepper. Sprinkle with green onions. Serve immediately.

BEANS AND LEGUMES

SOUTHWESTERN FLATBREAD

MAKES 4 SERVINGS

- 2 **oval flatbreads (about 11×7 inches)**
- ¼ **cup prepared green chile enchilada sauce**
- 2 **cups (8 ounces) shredded Monterey Jack cheese**
- 1 **can (about 14 ounces) black beans, rinsed and drained**
- 1 **cup frozen corn, thawed**
- ½ **cup finely chopped red onion**
- 1 **teaspoon olive oil**
- ½ **teaspoon salt**
- 1 **avocado, diced**
- 2 **tablespoons fresh chopped cilantro**
- **Lime wedges (optional)**

1 Preheat oven to 425°F. Place wire rack on large baking sheet; place flatbreads on rack.

2 Spread enchilada sauce over flatbreads; sprinkle with cheese. Combine beans, corn, onion, oil and salt in medium bowl; mix well. Spread mixture over cheese.

3 Bake 12 minutes or until flatbreads are golden and crisp and cheese is melted.

4 Sprinkle avocado over flatbreads; top with cilantro. Serve with lime wedges, if desired.

LENTIL BOLOGNESE

MAKES 6 TO 8 SERVINGS

2 tablespoons olive oil

1 onion, chopped

1 carrot, chopped

1 stalk celery, chopped

2 cloves garlic, minced

1 teaspoon salt

½ teaspoon dried oregano

Pinch red pepper flakes

3 tablespoons tomato
paste

¼ cup dry white wine

1 can (28 ounces) crushed
tomatoes

1 can (about 14 ounces)
diced tomatoes

1 cup dried lentils,
rinsed and sorted

1 portobello mushroom,
gills removed, finely
chopped

1½ cups water or vegetable
broth

Hot cooked pasta

1 Heat oil in large saucepan over medium heat. Add onion,
carrot and celery; cook and stir 10 minutes or until onion
is lightly browned and carrots are softened.

2 Stir in garlic, salt, oregano and red pepper flakes. Add
tomato paste; cook and stir 1 minute. Add wine; cook
and stir until absorbed. Stir in crushed tomatoes, diced
tomatoes, lentils, mushroom and water; bring to a
simmer.

3 Reduce heat to medium; partially cover and cook about
40 minutes or until lentils are tender, removing cover after
20 minutes. Serve sauce over pasta.

CHARRED CORN AND BLACK BEAN TACOS

MAKES 4 SERVINGS

1 **ear corn, husked**

1 **tablespoon plus 1 teaspoon olive oil, divided**

½ **teaspoon salt, plus additional for corn**

1 **small red onion, chopped**

1 **medium poblano pepper, chopped**

1 **clove garlic, minced**

½ **teaspoon ground cumin**

¼ **teaspoon dried oregano**

⅛ **teaspoon chipotle chili powder**

2 **tablespoons tomato paste**

1 **can (about 15 ounces) black beans, rinsed and drained**

¼ **cup water**

8 **taco-size flour or corn tortillas, warmed**

Spiced Sour Cream (recipe follows, optional)

Optional toppings: sliced avocado, thinly sliced chile pepper, shredded red cabbage, cotija cheese and fresh cilantro sprigs

1 Heat large cast iron skillet over medium-high heat. Brush corn with 1 teaspoon oil; sprinkle with salt. Cook about 10 minutes or until corn is charred on all sides, turning cob every few minutes to brown evenly.

2 Remove corn to cutting board; cut rows of kernels off cob with sharp knife.

3 Add remaining 1 tablespoon oil to same skillet; heat over medium-high heat. Add onion; cook about 6 minutes or until onion begins to turn golden brown, stirring occasionally. Add poblano; cook and stir 2 minutes. Add garlic, cumin, oregano, remaining ½ teaspoon salt and chipotle chili powder; cook and stir 1 minute. Add tomato paste; cook and stir 1 minute. Stir in beans and water; cook 5 minutes or until heated through.

4 Prepare Spiced Sour Cream, if desired. For each taco, spread scant ¼ cup bean mixture down center of tortilla; top with desired toppings. Serve with sour cream.

SPICED SOUR CREAM

Combine ½ cup sour cream, 2 teaspoons lime juice, ½ teaspoon salt, ⅛ teaspoon dried oregano and pinch of chipotle chili powder in small bowl; mix well.

PASTA E CECI

MAKES 4 SERVINGS

4 tablespoons olive oil, divided

1 onion, chopped

1 carrot, chopped

1 clove garlic, minced

1 sprig fresh rosemary

1 teaspoon salt

1 can (28 ounces) whole tomatoes, drained and crushed

2 cups vegetable broth or water

1 can (about 15 ounces) chickpeas, undrained

1 bay leaf

⅛ teaspoon red pepper flakes

1 cup uncooked orecchiette pasta

Black pepper

Chopped fresh parsley or basil

1 Heat 3 tablespoons oil in large saucepan over medium-high heat. Add onion and carrot; cook 10 minutes or until vegetables are softened, stirring occasionally.

2 Add garlic, rosemary and 1 teaspoon salt; cook and stir 1 minute. Stir in tomatoes, broth, chickpeas with liquid, bay leaf and red pepper flakes. Remove 1 cup mixture to food processor or blender; process until smooth. Stir mixture back into saucepan; bring to a boil.

3 Stir in pasta. Reduce heat to medium; cook 12 to 15 minutes or until pasta is tender and mixture is creamy. Remove and discard bay leaf and rosemary sprig. Taste and season with black pepper and additional salt, if desired.

4 Drizzle with remaining 1 tablespoon oil; garnish with parsley.

NOTE

To crush the tomatoes, take them out of the can one at a time and crush them between your fingers over the pot. Or coarsely chop them with a knife.

LENTIL BURGERS

MAKES 4 SERVINGS

1 **can (about 14 ounces) vegetable broth**

1 **cup dried lentils, rinsed and sorted**

1¼ **teaspoons salt, divided**

3 **tablespoons boiling water**

1 **tablespoon ground flaxseeds**

1 **small carrot, grated**

¼ **cup coarsely chopped mushrooms**

¼ **cup plain dry bread crumbs**

3 **tablespoons finely chopped onion**

2 **cloves garlic, minced**

1 **teaspoon dried thyme**

1 **tablespoon olive oil**

¼ **cup plain yogurt**

¼ **cup chopped seeded cucumber**

½ **teaspoon dried mint**

¼ **teaspoon dried dill weed**

¼ **teaspoon black pepper**

Kaiser rolls

Lettuce leaves

1 Bring broth to a boil in medium saucepan over high heat. Stir in lentils and 1 teaspoon salt. Reduce heat to low; cover and simmer about 30 minutes or until lentils are tender and liquid is absorbed. Cool to room temperature. Combine boiling water and flaxseeds in small bowl; let stand 10 minutes.

2 Combine lentils, carrot and mushrooms in food processor or blender; process until finely chopped but not smooth. (Some whole lentils should still be visible.) Stir in bread crumbs, onion, garlic, thyme and flaxseed mixture. Cover and refrigerate 2 to 3 hours.

3 Shape lentil mixture into 4 (½-inch-thick) patties. Heat oil in large nonstick skillet over medium-low heat. Cook patties about 5 minutes per side or until browned.

4 Meanwhile for sauce, combine yogurt, cucumber, mint, dill, black pepper and remaining ¼ teaspoon salt in small bowl; mix well. Serve burgers on rolls with lettuce and sauce.

ROASTED CHICKPEA AND SWEET POTATO BOWL

MAKES 2 SERVINGS

1 sweet potato (about 12 ounces)

1 tablespoon plus 1 teaspoon olive oil, divided

1 teaspoon salt, divided

Black pepper

1 can (about 15 ounces) chickpeas, rinsed and drained

1 tablespoon maple syrup

1 teaspoon paprika, sweet or smoked

½ teaspoon ground cumin

½ cup uncooked quinoa, rinsed

1 cup water

Chopped fresh parsley or cilantro

TAHINI SAUCE

¼ cup tahini

2 tablespoons lemon juice

2 tablespoons water

1 clove garlic, minced

⅛ teaspoon salt

1 Preheat oven to 350°F. Peel sweet potato; cut in half crosswise. Spiral sweet potato with thin ribbon blade of spiralizer. Cut into 3-inch pieces. (See Note.) Place in 13×9-inch baking pan. Drizzle with 1 teaspoon oil and sprinkle with ¼ teaspoon salt and black pepper; toss to coat. Push sweet potato to one side of pan.

2 Combine chickpeas, maple syrup, remaining 1 tablespoon oil, paprika, cumin and ½ teaspoon salt in medium bowl; toss to coat. Spread in other side of pan. Roast 30 minutes, stirring potatoes and chickpeas once or twice.

3 Meanwhile, rinse quinoa under cold water in fine-mesh strainer. Bring 1 cup water, quinoa and ¼ teaspoon salt to a boil in small saucepan over high heat. Reduce heat to low; cover and simmer 10 to 15 minutes or until quinoa is tender and water is absorbed.

4 For sauce, whisk tahini, lemon juice, 2 tablespoons water, garlic and ⅛ teaspoon salt in small bowl until smooth. Add additional water if needed to reach desired consistency.

5 Divide quinoa between two bowls; top with sweet potatoes, chickpeas and sauce. Sprinkle with parsley.

NOTE

If you don't have a spiralizer, cut the sweet potato into thin strips or ¼-inch cubes instead.

BLACK BEAN AND TEMPEH BURRITOS

MAKES 4 SERVINGS

1 tablespoon olive oil

½ cup chopped onion

½ cup chopped green bell pepper

2 cloves garlic, minced

2 teaspoons chili powder

2 cans (about 14 ounces each) stewed tomatoes

1 teaspoon dried oregano

½ teaspoon dried coriander

1 can (about 15 ounces) black beans, rinsed and drained

4 ounces tempeh, diced

¼ cup minced onion

¼ teaspoon black pepper

½ teaspoon ground cumin

8 (6-inch) flour tortillas

1 For sauce, heat oil in large nonstick skillet over medium heat. Add chopped onion, bell pepper and garlic; cook and stir 5 minutes or until onion is tender. Add chili powder; cook and stir 1 minute. Add tomatoes, oregano and coriander; cook 15 minutes, stirring occasionally.

2 Preheat oven to 350°F. Spray 13×9-inch baking dish with nonstick cooking spray. Place beans in medium bowl; mash with fork. Add tempeh, minced onion, black pepper and cumin; mix well. Stir in ¼ cup sauce.

3 Soften tortillas if necessary.* Spread ⅓ cup bean mixture down center of each tortilla. Roll up tortillas; place in single layer in prepared baking dish. Top with remaining sauce.

4 Bake 15 minutes or until heated through.

*To soften tortillas, wrap stack of tortillas in foil. Heat in preheated 350°F oven about 10 minutes or until softened.

PICANTE PINTOS AND RICE

MAKES 8 SERVINGS

2 cups dried pinto beans, rinsed and sorted

2 cups water

1 can (about 14 ounces) stewed tomatoes

1 cup coarsely chopped onion

¾ cup coarsely chopped green bell pepper

¼ cup sliced celery

4 cloves garlic, minced

½ small jalapeño pepper,* seeded and chopped

2 teaspoons dried oregano

2 teaspoons chili powder

½ teaspoon ground red pepper

2 cups chopped kale

1 teaspoon salt

4 cups hot cooked brown rice

Jalapeño peppers can sting and irritate the skin, so wear rubber gloves when handling peppers and do not touch your eyes.

1 Place beans in large saucepan; add water to cover by 2 inches. Bring to a boil over high heat; boil 2 minutes. Remove from heat; cover and let stand 1 hour. Drain beans; return to saucepan.

2 Add 2 cups water, tomatoes, onion, bell pepper, celery, garlic, jalapeño, oregano, chili powder and ground red pepper to saucepan; bring to a boil over high heat. Reduce heat to low; cook, uncovered, about 1½ hours or until beans are tender, stirring occasionally.

3 Stir in kale and salt; cook 30 minutes, stirring occasionally. (Beans will be very tender.) Serve over rice.

CHUNKY BLACK BEAN AND SWEET POTATO CHILI

MAKES 4 SERVINGS

- 1 tablespoon grapeseed oil
- 1 cup chopped sweet onion
- 2 red or green bell peppers (or 1 of each), cut into ½-inch pieces
- 4 cloves garlic, minced
- 1 teaspoon chili powder
- ½ teaspoon salt
- 1 can (about 14 ounces) fire-roasted diced tomatoes
- 1 small sweet potato (8 ounces), peeled and cut into ½-inch chunks (1½ cups)
- 1 tablespoon minced canned chipotle pepper in adobo sauce
- 1 can (about 15 ounces) black beans, rinsed and drained
- ½ cup chopped fresh cilantro (optional)

1 Heat oil in large saucepan over medium heat. Add onion; cook and stir 5 minutes. Add bell peppers, garlic, chili powder and salt; cook and stir 2 minutes. Add tomatoes, sweet potato and chipotle pepper; bring to a boil. Reduce heat to medium-low; cover and cook 15 minutes.

2 Stir in beans; cover and cook 8 to 10 minutes or until vegetables are tender. (Chili will be thick; thin with water as desired.)

3 Top with cilantro, if desired.

VEGETABLE BEAN QUESADILLAS

MAKES 8 SERVINGS

1 tablespoon olive oil

1 cup sliced onion

1 can (about 15 ounces) black beans, rinsed and drained

1 cup sliced green bell pepper

1 cup sliced red bell pepper

½ teaspoon ground cumin

¼ teaspoon salt

¼ teaspoon ground red pepper

8 (8-inch) whole grain tortillas

1 cup (4 ounces) shredded Cheddar cheese

Salsa (optional)

1 Heat oil in large skillet over medium-high heat. Add onion; cook and stir 3 minutes or until translucent. Add beans, bell peppers, cumin, salt and ground red pepper; cook and stir 3 minutes or until bell peppers are crisp-tender.

2 Heat medium nonstick skillet over medium heat. Place 1 tortilla in skillet. Spread about ⅓ cup vegetables on half of tortilla; sprinkle with 2 tablespoons cheese. Fold tortilla over filling; cook until bottom is lightly browned. Turn and brown other side. Fill and cook remaining tortillas.

3 Cut into wedges. Serve with salsa, if desired.

CHICKPEA BURGERS

MAKES 4 SERVINGS

1 can (about 15 ounces) chickpeas, rinsed and drained

⅓ cup chopped carrots

⅓ cup herbed croutons

¼ cup chopped fresh parsley

¼ cup chopped onion

1 egg

1 teaspoon minced garlic

1 teaspoon grated lemon peel

½ teaspoon salt

½ teaspoon black pepper

1 tablespoon olive oil

4 whole grain hamburger buns

Tomato slices, lettuce leaves and salsa (optional)

1 Combine chickpeas, carrots, croutons, parsley, onion, egg, garlic, lemon peel, salt and pepper in food processor; process until blended. Shape mixture into 4 patties.

2 Heat oil in large nonstick skillet over medium heat. Cook patties 4 to 5 minutes or until bottoms are browned. Turn and cook 4 to 5 minutes or until browned.

3 Serve burgers on buns with tomato, lettuce and salsa, if desired.

ZESTY VEGETARIAN CHILI
MAKES 4 SERVINGS

1 tablespoon grapeseed oil

1 large red bell pepper, coarsely chopped

2 medium zucchini or yellow squash (or 1 of each), cut into ½-inch pieces

4 cloves garlic, minced

1 can (about 14 ounces) fire-roasted diced tomatoes

¾ cup chunky salsa

2 teaspoons chili powder

1 teaspoon dried oregano

½ teaspoon salt

1 can (about 15 ounces) red kidney beans, rinsed and drained

10 ounces extra firm tofu, well drained and cut into ½-inch cubes

Chopped fresh cilantro (optional)

1 Heat oil in large saucepan over medium heat. Add bell pepper; cook and stir 4 minutes. Add zucchini and garlic; cook and stir 3 minutes.

2 Stir in tomatoes, salsa, chili powder, oregano and salt; bring to a boil over high heat. Reduce heat to low; cook 15 minutes or until vegetables are tender.

3 Stir in beans; cook 2 minutes or until heated through. Gently stir in tofu; cook 1 minute. Garnish with cilantro.

MEDITERRANEAN PITA SANDWICHES
MAKES 4 SERVINGS

1 **cup plain yogurt**

1 **tablespoon chopped fresh cilantro**

2 **cloves garlic, minced**

1 **teaspoon lemon juice**

¼ **teaspoon salt**

1 **can (about 15 ounces) chickpeas, rinsed and drained**

1 **can (14 ounces) artichoke hearts, rinsed, drained and coarsely chopped**

1½ **cups thinly sliced cucumber (halved lengthwise)**

½ **cup shredded carrot**

½ **cup chopped green onions**

4 **whole wheat pita bread rounds, cut in half**

1 Combine yogurt, cilantro, garlic, lemon juice and salt in small bowl; mix well.

2 Combine chickpeas, artichokes, cucumber, carrot and green onions in medium bowl. Add yogurt mixture; stir gently to coat.

3 Serve chickpea mixture in pita halves.

VEGETABLES

ROASTED FENNEL AND SPAGHETTI

MAKES 2 TO 4 SERVINGS

2 bulbs fennel, trimmed, cored and sliced ¼-inch thick

2 carrots, peeled and quartered

2 tablespoons plus 1 teaspoon olive oil, divided

½ teaspoon salt, divided

¼ teaspoon black pepper

1 cup fresh bread crumbs

2 cloves garlic, minced

8 ounces uncooked spaghetti

2 tablespoons lemon juice

2 tablespoons chopped fresh oregano

1 Preheat oven to 400°F. Combine fennel and carrots on baking sheet. Drizzle with 1 tablespoon oil and sprinkle with ¼ teaspoon salt and pepper; toss to coat. Spread vegetables in single layer on baking sheet.

2 Roast 30 minutes or until vegetables are tender and well browned, stirring once or twice. When carrots are cool enough to handle, cut diagonally into 1-inch pieces.

3 Meanwhile, heat 1 tablespoon oil in medium skillet over medium heat. Add bread crumbs and garlic; cook and stir about 3 minutes or until bread is toasted. Remove from heat; stir in remaining ¼ teaspoon salt.

4 Cook pasta in large saucepan of salted water according to package directions until al dente. Drain and return to saucepan. Stir in lemon juice and remaining 1 teaspoon oil. Divide pasta among serving bowls; top with vegetables, bread crumbs and oregano.

CRISPY SMASHED POTATOES

MAKES ABOUT 6 SERVINGS

1 tablespoon plus ½ teaspoon salt, divided

3 pounds unpeeled small red potatoes (2 inches or smaller)

4 tablespoons (½ stick) butter, melted, divided

¼ teaspoon black pepper

½ cup grated Parmesan cheese (optional)

1 Fill large saucepan three-fourths full of water; add 1 tablespoon salt. Bring to a boil over medium-high heat. Add potatoes; cook about 20 minutes or until potatoes are tender when pierced with tip of sharp knife. Drain potatoes; set aside until cool enough to handle.

2 Preheat oven to 450°F. Brush baking sheet with 2 tablespoons butter. Working with one potato at a time, smash with hand or bottom of measuring cup to about ½-inch thickness. Arrange smashed potatoes in single layer on prepared baking sheet. Brush with remaining 2 tablespoons butter; sprinkle with remaining ½ teaspoon salt and pepper.

3 Bake 30 to 40 minutes or until bottoms of potatoes are golden brown. Turn potatoes; bake 10 to 15 minutes or until golden brown. Sprinkle with cheese, if desired.

CAULIFLOWER TACOS WITH CHIPOTLE CREMA

MAKES 8 TACOS (4 SERVINGS)

Pickled Red Onions (recipe follows) or chopped red onion

1 **package (8 ounces) sliced cremini mushrooms**

4 **tablespoons olive oil, divided**

1½ **teaspoons salt, divided**

1 **head cauliflower**

1 **teaspoon ground cumin**

½ **teaspoon dried oregano**

¼ **teaspoon ground coriander**

¼ **teaspoon ground cinnamon**

¼ **teaspoon black pepper**

½ **cup sour cream or plain Greek yogurt**

2 **teaspoons lime juice**

½ **teaspoon chipotle chili powder**

½ **cup vegetarian refried beans**

8 **taco-size flour or corn tortillas**

Chopped fresh cilantro

Pickled Red Onions (recipe follows) or chopped red onion

1 Prepare Pickled Red Onions. Preheat oven to 400°F. Combine mushrooms, 1 tablespoon oil and ¼ teaspoon salt in large bowl; toss to coat. Spread on small baking sheet.

2 Remove leaves from cauliflower. Remove florets; cut into 1-inch pieces. Place in same large bowl. Add remaining 3 tablespoons oil, 1 teaspoon salt, cumin, oregano, coriander, cinnamon and black pepper; mix well. Spread in single layer on large baking sheet.

3 Roast cauliflower about 40 minutes or until browned and tender, stirring several times. Roast mushrooms 20 minutes or until dry and browned, stirring once.

4 For crema, combine sour cream, lime juice, chipotle chili powder and remaining ¼ teaspoon salt in small bowl; mix well.

5 For each taco, spread 1 tablespoon beans over tortilla; spread 1 teaspoon crema over beans. Top with about 3 mushroom slices and ¼ cup cauliflower. Top with cilantro and pickled onions. Fold in half.

PICKLED RED ONIONS

Thinly slice 1 small red onion; place in large glass jar. Add ¼ cup white wine vinegar or distilled white vinegar, 2 tablespoons water, 1 teaspoon sugar and 1 teaspoon salt. Seal jar; shake well. Refrigerate at least 1 hour or up to 1 week.

MEDITERRANEAN-STYLE ROASTED VEGETABLES

MAKES 6 SERVINGS

1½ pounds red potatoes, cut into ½-inch pieces

2 tablespoons olive oil, divided

1 red bell pepper, cut into ½-inch pieces

1 yellow or orange bell pepper, cut into ½-inch pieces

1 small red onion, cut into ½-inch wedges

2 cloves garlic, minced

1 teaspoon salt

¼ teaspoon black pepper

1 tablespoon balsamic vinegar

¼ cup chopped fresh basil leaves

1 Preheat oven to 425°F. Spray large roasting pan or baking sheet with nonstick cooking spray.

2 Place potatoes in prepared pan. Drizzle with 1 tablespoon oil; toss to coat. Roast 10 minutes.

3 Add bell peppers and onion to pan; drizzle with remaining 1 tablespoon oil. Sprinkle with garlic, salt and black pepper; toss to coat.

4 Roast 18 to 20 minutes or until vegetables are browned and tender, stirring once.

5 Transfer vegetables to large serving dish. Drizzle with vinegar; toss to coat. Add basil; toss again. Serve warm or at room temperature.

TOMATO MOZZARELLA SANDWICH

MAKES 4 SERVINGS

BALSAMIC VINAIGRETTE

6 tablespoons extra virgin olive oil

3 tablespoons balsamic vinegar

1 clove garlic, minced

1 teaspoon honey

1 teaspoon Dijon mustard

½ teaspoon dried oregano

½ teaspoon salt

⅛ teaspoon black pepper

SANDWICHES

1 baguette, ends trimmed, cut into 4 equal pieces (4 ounces each) and split

1 cup loosely packed baby arugula

3 medium tomatoes, sliced ¼ inch thick

1 cup roasted red peppers, patted dry and thinly sliced

12 slices fresh mozzarella (one 8-ounce package)

12 fresh basil leaves

1 For vinaigrette, whisk oil, vinegar, garlic, honey, mustard, oregano, salt and pepper in small bowl until well blended.

2 For each sandwich, drizzle 1 tablespoon vinaigrette over bottom half of bread. Layer with arugula, tomatoes, roasted peppers, cheese, additional arugula and basil. Drizzle with 1 tablespoon dressing; replace top half of bread.

BALSAMIC BUTTERNUT SQUASH

MAKES 4 SERVINGS

3 tablespoons olive oil

2 tablespoons thinly sliced fresh sage (about 6 large leaves), divided

1 medium butternut squash, peeled and cut into 1-inch pieces (4 to 5 cups)

½ red onion, cut in half and cut into ¼-inch slices

1 teaspoon salt, divided

2½ tablespoons balsamic vinegar

¼ teaspoon black pepper

1 Heat oil in large cast iron skillet over medium-high heat. Add 1 tablespoon sage; cook and stir 3 minutes. Add squash, onion and ½ teaspoon salt; cook 6 minutes, stirring occasionally. Reduce heat to medium; cook 15 minutes without stirring.

2 Stir in vinegar, remaining ½ teaspoon salt and pepper; cook 10 minutes or until squash is tender, stirring occasionally. Stir in remaining 1 tablespoon sage; cook 1 minute.

SPINACH VEGGIE WRAP
MAKES 4 SERVINGS

PICO DE GALLO

- **1 cup finely chopped tomatoes (about 2 small)**
- **½ teaspoon salt**
- **¼ cup chopped white onion**
- **2 tablespoons minced jalapeño pepper**
- **2 tablespoons chopped fresh cilantro**
- **1 teaspoon lime juice**

GUACAMOLE

- **2 large ripe avocados**
- **¼ cup finely chopped red onion**
- **2 tablespoons chopped fresh cilantro**
- **2 teaspoons lime juice**
- **½ teaspoon salt**

WRAPS

- **4 (10-inch) whole wheat tortillas**
- **2 cups baby spinach**
- **1 cup sliced mushrooms**
- **1 cup shredded Asiago cheese**
- **Salsa**

1. For pico de gallo, combine tomatoes and ½ teaspoon salt in fine-mesh strainer; set over bowl to drain 15 minutes. Combine drained tomatoes, white onion, jalapeño, 2 tablespoons cilantro and 1 teaspoon lime juice in medium bowl; mix well.

2. For guacamole, combine avocados, red onion, 2 tablespoons cilantro, 2 teaspoons lime juice and ½ teaspoon salt in medium bowl; mash with fork to desired consistency.

3. For wraps, spread ¼ cup guacamole on each tortilla. Layer each with ½ cup spinach, ¼ cup mushrooms, ¼ cup cheese and ¼ cup pico de gallo. Roll up; serve with salsa.

ROASTED CURRIED CAULIFLOWER AND BRUSSELS SPROUTS

MAKES 10 SERVINGS

2	**pounds cauliflower florets**
12	**ounces Brussels sprouts, cleaned and cut in half**
⅓	**cup olive oil**
½	**teaspoon sea salt**
½	**teaspoon black pepper**
2½	**tablespoons curry powder**
½	**cup chopped fresh cilantro**

1 Preheat oven to 400°F. Line large baking sheet with foil.

2 Combine cauliflower, Brussels sprouts and oil in large bowl; toss to coat. Sprinkle with salt, pepper and curry powder; toss to coat. Spread vegetables in single layer on prepared baking sheet.

3 Roast 20 to 25 minutes or until vegetables are golden brown, stirring after 15 minutes.

4 Add cilantro; toss until blended.

MUSHROOM AND VEGETABLE RAGOÛT OVER POLENTA

MAKES 6 SERVINGS

RAGOÛT

- **3 tablespoons olive oil**
- **8 ounces sliced mushrooms**
- **8 ounces shiitake mushrooms, stemmed and thinly sliced**
- **½ cup Madeira wine**
- **1 can (28 ounces) crushed tomatoes**
- **1 can (about 15 ounces) chickpeas, rinsed and drained**
- **1 medium onion, chopped**
- **1 can (about 6 ounces) tomato paste**
- **4 cloves garlic, minced**
- **1 sprig fresh rosemary**
- **½ teaspoon salt**

POLENTA

- **2 cups whole milk**
- **2 cups water**
- **¼ teaspoon salt**
- **1 cup instant polenta**
- **½ cup grated Parmesan cheese**

SLOW COOKER DIRECTIONS

1 For ragoût, heat oil in large skillet over medium-high heat. Add mushrooms; cook and stir 8 to 10 minutes or until browned. Add Madeira; cook 1 minute or until liquid is reduced by half. Transfer to slow cooker. Stir in tomatoes, chickpeas, onion, tomato paste, garlic, rosemary and ½ teaspoon salt; mix well.

2 Cover; cook on LOW 6 hours or until vegetables are tender. Remove and discard rosemary sprig.

3 For polenta, combine milk, water and ¼ teaspoon salt in large saucepan; bring to a boil over medium-high heat. Slowly whisk in polenta in slow, steady stream. Cook 4 to 5 minutes or until thick and creamy, whisking constantly.

4 Remove from heat; stir in cheese. Serve polenta with ragoût.

TOFU, VEGETABLE AND CURRY STIR-FRY

MAKES 4 SERVINGS

- 1 package (14 ounces) extra firm tofu, cut into ¾-inch cubes
- ¾ cup coconut milk
- 2 tablespoons lime juice
- 1 tablespoon curry powder
- ½ teaspoon salt
- 2 teaspoons dark sesame oil, divided
- 4 cups broccoli florets (1½-inch pieces)
- 2 medium red bell peppers, cut into short, thin strips
- 1 medium red onion, cut into thin wedges

  Hot cooked brown rice (optional)

1 Press tofu cubes between layers of paper towels to remove excess moisture. Combine coconut milk, lime juice, curry powder and salt in medium bowl; mix well.

2 Heat 1 teaspoon oil in large nonstick skillet over medium heat. Add tofu; cook 10 minutes or until lightly browned on all sides, turning frequently. Remove to plate.

3 Add remaining 1 teaspoon oil to skillet. Add broccoli, bell peppers and onion; stir-fry over high heat about 5 minutes or until vegetables are crisp-tender. Stir in tofu and coconut milk mixture; bring to a boil, stirring frequently. Serve immediately with rice, if desired.

BUTTERNUT SQUASH OVEN FRIES

MAKES 4 SERVINGS

½ **teaspoon garlic powder**

¼ **teaspoon salt**

¼ **teaspoon ground red pepper**

1 **butternut squash (about 2½ pounds), peeled, seeded and cut into 2-inch-thin slices**

2 **teaspoons vegetable oil**

1 Preheat oven to 425°F. Combine garlic powder, salt and red pepper in small bowl; mix well.

2 Place squash on baking sheet. Drizzle with oil and sprinkle with seasoning mix; toss gently to coat. Spread in single layer on baking sheet.

3 Bake 20 to 25 minutes or until squash just begins to brown, stirring frequently. Preheat broiler.

4 Broil 3 to 5 minutes or until fries are browned and crisp. Cool slightly before serving.

MEDITERRANEAN ROASTED VEGETABLE WRAPS

MAKES 4 SERVINGS

1 head cauliflower, cut into 1-inch florets

4 tablespoons plus 2 teaspoons olive oil, divided

2 teaspoons ras el hanout, 7-spice blend, shawarma blend or za'atar

1 teaspoon salt, divided

1 zucchini, quartered lengthwise and cut into ¼-inch pieces

1 yellow squash, quartered lengthwise and cut into ¼-inch pieces

½ red onion, thinly sliced

¼ cup red pepper sauce (avjar)

4 large thin pita bread rounds or lavash (10 inches)

4 ounces feta cheese, crumbled

1 cup chickpeas

¼ cup diced tomatoes

¼ cup minced fresh parsley

¼ cup diced cucumber (optional)

2 teaspoons olive oil

1 Preheat oven to 400°F. Combine cauliflower, 2 tablespoons oil, ras el hanout and ½ teaspoon salt in large bowl; toss to coat. Spread on half of baking sheet. Combine zucchini, yellow squash, onion, 2 tablespoons oil and remaining ½ teaspoon salt in same bowl; toss to coat. Spread on other side of baking sheet.

2 Roast 25 minutes or until vegetables are browned and tender, stirring once. Remove from oven; cool slightly.

3 Spread 1 tablespoon red pepper sauce on one pita bread. Top with one fourth of vegetables, cheese, chickpeas, tomatoes, parsley and cucumber, if desired. Fold two sides over filling; roll up into burrito shape. Repeat with remaining ingredients.

4 Heat 1 teaspoon oil in large skillet over medium-high heat. Add two wraps, seam sides down; cook 1 minute or until browned. Turn and cook other side until browned. Repeat with remaining oil and wraps. Cut in half to serve.

BARLEY AND VEGETABLE RISOTTO

MAKES 4 SERVINGS

4½ **cups vegetable broth**

1 **tablespoon olive oil**

1 **small onion, chopped**

8 **ounces sliced mushrooms**

¾ **cup uncooked pearl barley**

1 **large red bell pepper, diced**

2 **cups packed baby spinach**

½ **cup grated Parmesan cheese**

¼ **teaspoon black pepper**

1 Bring broth to a boil in medium saucepan over high heat. Reduce heat to low to maintain a simmer.

2 Meanwhile, heat oil in large saucepan over medium heat. Add onion; cook and stir 4 minutes. Add mushrooms; cook over medium-high heat 5 minutes or until mushrooms begin to brown and liquid evaporates, stirring frequently.

3 Add barley; cook 1 minute. Add broth, ¼ cup at a time, stirring constantly until broth is almost absorbed before adding the next ¼ cup. After 20 minutes of cooking, stir in bell pepper. Continue adding broth, ¼ cup at a time, until barley is tender (about 30 minutes total).

4 Stir in spinach; cook and stir 1 minute or just until spinach is wilted. Stir in cheese and black pepper.

TIP

Use your favorite mushrooms, such as button, crimini or shiitake, or a combination of two or more varieties.

METRIC CONVERSION CHART

VOLUME MEASUREMENTS (dry)

1/8 teaspoon = 0.5 mL
1/4 teaspoon = 1 mL
1/2 teaspoon = 2 mL
3/4 teaspoon = 4 mL
1 teaspoon = 5 mL
1 tablespoon = 15 mL
2 tablespoons = 30 mL
1/4 cup = 60 mL
1/3 cup = 75 mL
1/2 cup = 125 mL
2/3 cup = 150 mL
3/4 cup = 175 mL
1 cup = 250 mL
2 cups = 1 pint = 500 mL
3 cups = 750 mL
4 cups = 1 quart = 1 L

VOLUME MEASUREMENTS (fluid)

1 fluid ounce (2 tablespoons) = 30 mL
4 fluid ounces (1/2 cup) = 125 mL
8 fluid ounces (1 cup) = 250 mL
12 fluid ounces (1 1/2 cups) = 375 mL
16 fluid ounces (2 cups) = 500 mL

WEIGHTS (mass)

1/2 ounce = 15 g
1 ounce = 30 g
3 ounces = 90 g
4 ounces = 120 g
8 ounces = 225 g
10 ounces = 285 g
12 ounces = 360 g
16 ounces = 1 pound = 450 g

DIMENSIONS

1/16 inch = 2 mm
1/8 inch = 3 mm
1/4 inch = 6 mm
1/2 inch = 1.5 cm
3/4 inch = 2 cm
1 inch = 2.5 cm

OVEN TEMPERATURES

250°F = 120°C
275°F = 140°C
300°F = 150°C
325°F = 160°C
350°F = 180°C
375°F = 190°C
400°F = 200°C
425°F = 220°C
450°F = 230°C

BAKING PAN SIZES

Utensil	Size in Inches/Quarts	Metric Volume	Size in Centimeters
Baking or Cake Pan (square or rectangular)	8×8×2	2 L	20×20×5
	9×9×2	2.5 L	23×23×5
	12×8×2	3 L	30×20×5
	13×9×2	3.5 L	33×23×5
Loaf Pan	8×4×3	1.5 L	20×10×7
	9×5×3	2 L	23×13×7
Round Layer Cake Pan	8×1½	1.2 L	20×4
	9×1½	1.5 L	23×4
Pie Plate	8×1¼	750 mL	20×3
	9×1¼	1 L	23×3
Baking Dish or Casserole	1 quart	1 L	—
	1½ quart	1.5 L	—
	2 quart	2 L	—